LOLA Light in Hand RIDGE

LOLA Light

in Hand
RIDGE

Selected Early Poems
Edited by Daniel Tobin

Quale Press

"Modernism, Leftism, and the Spirit: The Poetry of Lola Ridge" previously appeared in somewhat different form in the *New Hibernia Review* 8:3 (Autumn/Winter 2004), pages 65–85.

Cover and Interior Design by Jessica Phillips

Background photo for cover: "Tenement dwellers dropping clothes from fire escape for Italians on East Side, New York," 1909, Bain News Service, courtesy of the George Grantham Bain Collection at the Library of Congress

ISBN: 978–0–9792999–1–9
LCCN: 2007923325

Quale Press
www.quale.com

CONTENTS

THE GHETTO
AND OTHER POEMS

SUN-UP
AND OTHER POEMS

RED FLAG

MODERISM, LEFTISM, AND THE SPIRIT
The Poetry of Lola Ridge

Born Rose Emily Ridge in Dublin on December 12,1873, the woman who would reinvent herself to become perhaps the most impassioned and certainly the most authentic of the proletarian poets of the New York modernist avant-garde emigrated with her mother as a child to New Zealand where she would marry the manager of a gold mine at the age of twenty-one. To look ahead thirty years from the life she had chosen in 1895 is to gain some measure of insight into the transformation she had undergone. In 1927, Alfred Kreymborg—one of the leading avant-garde poets of the day—describes her as "the frailest of humans physically and the poorest financially," though nevertheless, as Peter Quatermain remarks, she was a "woman on the spiritual barricade fighting with her pen against tyranny."[1] Indeed, after her marriage to Peter Webster failed and her mother died, Lola Ridge emigrated to the United States in 1907, staying for a brief time in California, then settling in Manhattan's Greenwich Village. So began her life as one of the multitudes of left-wing reformers and artists (among them Kay Boyle, John Dos Passos, Harold Loeb, and Emma Goldman) who moved to lower Manhattan and contributed to its hot-bed of activism. Indeed, throughout the nineteenth century lower Manhattan had filled with poor immigrants and workers supportive of leftist causes. As an activist of revolutionary fervor, over the next three decades until her death in Brooklyn in 1941, Ridge nevertheless composed some of the most vivid and politically conscious poems of her day. At the same time, her presence among New York's avant-garde places her work within the context of such luminaries of modernist American poetry as Marianne Moore, William Carlos Williams, and Hart Crane. The peripatetic literary and cultural sojourns of "The Lost Generation," to which Ridge also had strong if contentious ties, also provide an evocative counterpoint to both the literary and civic life she herself decided to lead, as do the right-wing modernist programs of expatriate mandarins Ezra Pound and T. S. Eliot, and the pure poetries of the Dadaists. From this perspective, Ridge appears to be a notable lone figure standing amidst the crowd of our American literary history, at once recognizable in the aesthetic and wider cultural currents of her time, but nevertheless curiously otherwise—a vivid original whose life and work embody the tumultuous confluence of forces that shaped the twentieth century.

To picture Lola Ridge as a defiant and heroic loner is not to engage in a kind of romanticism that she herself would refuse to embrace. Like Yeats without the imaginative infrastructure of a spiritual system, by the time she arrived in San Francisco and moved to Greenwich Village Ridge had already invented an "idealized version of herself."[2] "Rose Emily" had become "Lola," a woman ten years younger than her actual age, as well as a poet, artist, and revolutionary. In this regard she reminds one of another "Lola"—Lola Montez, born Maria Delores Eliza Rosanna Gilbert in Limerick in 1824 before recreating herself as the Spanish "Spider Dancer" and nineteenth-century America's embodiment of immodesty. Both women were Irish emigrants who were forced to rely on their own powers of self-imagination to establish places for themselves in their respective worlds; both became famous in their time; both turned to religion and embraced the plight of the poor and the outcast. Unlike Montez, however, whose beauty and sensuality were legendary, Ridge assumed the visage of a saint and ascetic. Tall and thin, "frail enough to be blown away like a leaf"[3] according to Kay Boyle, blood-drained, her body slowly wasting with pulmonary tuberculosis, the image of Ridge as an impassioned and even saintly idealist emerges in Katherine Anne Porter's description of the protest outside Charlestown Prison in Boston on August 22, 1927, where Sacco and Vanzetti, a shoemaker and a fish-peddler, both avowed anarchists, were to be executed the next day for a payroll robbery and murder committed seven years earlier. Many believed them innocent, and that execution would be martyrdom for their political beliefs. As the police at the protest galloped about on horseback, "bearing down" as Porter tells us "on anyone who ventured beyond the edge of the crowd... one tall, thin figure of a woman stepped out alone, a good distance into the empty square, and when the police came down on her and the horse's hoofs beat over her head, she did not move, but stood with her shoulders slightly bowed, entirely still."[4] The woman was Lola Ridge. So dramatic a commitment to her political and social ideals was not uncommon, nor was it alien to her artistic temperament. Horace Gregory, like Kay Boyle another Irish American with a substantial literary future, described their mutual friend as legendary in her "austere devotion to her talents."[5] Indeed, beyond linking the intensity of Ridge's verve for social justice to her poetry, Gregory declares that "Ridge was possessed of a Celtic imagination whose insights gave life and color to her convictions."[6] He goes still further to portray Ridge as "unworldly," a "vision-haunted Irish heroine" whose wind-swept, cold-water loft in the Village "was like some neatly, frugally kept cold-water flat in Dublin."

While one ought to take Gregory's perhaps overly romanticized portrayal of Ridge and his presuppositions about a Celtic imagination with a grain of salt, there is no doubt that the fervency of Ridge's embrace of the life of deliberate poverty and her devotion to making poems both artistically vital and mindful of the poor and oppressed have their origins at least in part in her sense of identity as someone born Irish and therefore the inheritor of a particularly passionate and tragic cultural experience. Her passion for social justice finds an explicitly Irish expression in her poems dedicated to James Larkin, the great labor organizer, and Kevin Barry, a model of idealism in the face of force and a martyr to British oppression during the war for Irish independence. Her devotion to Ireland comes nearest to Gregory's belief in a Celtic imagination in her poem "The Tidings," written on the occasion of the Easter Rising. There, with a longing reminiscent and perhaps derivative of Francis Ledwidge's in the trenches of France, she writes, "My heart is like a lover foiled / By a broken stair— / *They are fighting to-night in Sackville Street, / and I am not there!*"[7] She broaches the subject of Ireland again, now symbolically, in the poem "Incompatability" from her third book, *Red Flag*:

> Bull's-hide white under red wrath
> And a curt tone of blue...
> By a gold harp on a green cloth—
> How should they blend, these two?[8]

Though long departed from Ireland, Ridge's poem places her concern with the country of her birth and its continued dominance by John Bull's Union Jack in a volume that promotes its leftist sensibility in its title. At the same time, given the image of Ridge's willingness to undergo a potential martyrdom under the horse's hooves at Charlestown Prison, and the increasingly mystical tenor of her poetry in the books that followed *Red Flag*, her work also at times comes to echo the spiritual radicalism of Padraic Pearse—"O King that was born / To set bondsmen free / In the coming battle / Help the Gael!"[9] Ridge would write her own poem, the epic *Firehead*, to dramatize the life of that King. Moreover, as Kay Boyle recounts, Ridge's advocacy of suffering as a means to achieve redemption—not merely of the individual soul but of the world—greatly influenced her during the formative years of her own artistic and imagination growth. "Lola's causes became mine," Boyle writes,

> and when I wrote my poems now I borrowed from her conscience and her poetic vocabulary. She gave to my rebellion a wider and, at the same time, a more indigenous setting. For a long time my heart had bled with the Irish insurgents, and I had carried everywhere with me a copy of Terrence MacSwiney's letter to Cathal Brugha, a letter which he... had written after forty-six days of hunger striking...
>
> The reason for MacSwiney's death had defined for me in clearest terms the rebellion of the flesh against organized authority... But now it was Lola who spoke the vocabulary I wanted to hear, and all I had cherished

vicariously took on the shadowy dimensions of another country's history.[10]

Clearly, for the young Kay Boyle, Lola Ridge had become the embodiment of a specifically Irish dedication to a rebellion against injustice that was at once spiritual and worldly, as well as a mother figure at once associated with her own mother and with the Virgin.[11] Still more significantly, as the daughter of Irish immigrants Boyle envisions the spiritually fueled "rebellion of the flesh against authority" as an ideal to put into practice in the New World, a legacy to be carried over from "another country's history." Ridge surely envisioned her connection to this tradition along similar lines, though at the same time the uniquely American context displayed in the majority of her poems reveals the forward-looking direction of her work. Her imagination is not merely Celtic, as Horace Gregory would have it, but emigrant in its character. One need only read her long poem, "The Ghetto," a sustained portrait of life in the Jewish-American ghetto where she lived, or the ironic "Lullaby" in which an African American baby is thrown into a burning house by a white woman, to recognize that Ridge harbors no nostalgia either for "Inisfail" or "The Land Paved With Gold." Indeed, her implicit affirmation of an Irish American poetic consciousness in poems like "Crucible," written in praise of Robinson Jeffers, as well as in her affiliation and support of such younger poets as Horace Gregory and especially Kay Boyle, bears witness to her desire to forge both a life and a body of work at once resonant with Irish traditions though nonetheless cast in the American grain.

By all accounts, the literary and artistic crucible of New York's avant-garde salons in the 1920s composed a striking mix of personalities and sensibilities, and Ridge quickly assumed a prominent if often circumspect position in that world. In February 1922, she became the American editor of *Broom*. Edited from Rome by expatriate New Yorker Harold Loeb, *Broom* sought to be the foremost journal of its day—indeed, *the* journal of cultural note—publishing work by Alfred Kreymborg, Kenneth Burke, Robert McAlmon, Ernest Walsh, Gertrude Stein, Malcolm Cowley, and a host of other writers, a few of whom (like Marianne Moore, William Carlos Williams, and Hart Crane) would eventually enter the canon of American literature. Part of Ridge's duties as American editor was to host a literary salon on Thursday afternoons with her second husband David Lawson, where the likes of Kay Boyle, John Dos Passos, Mina Loy, Glenway Wescott, Jean Toomer, Edward Arlington Robinson, Marianne Moore, and William Carlos Williams would read their work and discuss artistic and literary trends. "We had arguments over cubism that would fill an afternoon," William Carlos Williams recounts in his *Autobiography*.[12] For her part, Kay Boyle observes in *Being Geniuses Together* that Ridge inspired sharply divided responses among those attending the salon. For Boyle, Ridge's commitment both to the poor and her art brought her near to sainthood. "I cherished and protected her as if she were a small bright flame," Boyle recounts. "Her work expressed a fiery awareness of social injustice as eloquently as Emanuel Carnevali's or Maxwell Bodenheim's, but it was always Lola's voice that spoke, a woman's savage voice, not theirs..."[13] In contrast, by Boyle's own admission, Robert McAlmon "had little sympathy for Lola's earnest commitment to the arts and to the working class, a commitment so dramatized that people felt the necessity of either defending or abusing her whenever her name came up."[14] William Carlos Williams sums up the manner in which Ridge presided over the salon rather tersely and ironically but no doubt perceptively given the intensity of her social, artistic, and spiritual beliefs—"She made a religion of it."[15] Matthew Josephson, a would-be poet and associate of Harold Loeb's, in his *Life Among the Surrealists* dismisses her time and again as "difficult" and condescends to her editorial abilities when he recounts that the European editors rejected most of the writers she recommended.[16] Loeb objected to her "hair-trigger judgments and dogmatic opinions."[17] To be sure, it appears that Ridge was difficult in the way all passionate artists and social advocates are difficult when their sensibilities clash with those of others, and especially those in power. Ridge often took no salary for her work on *Broom*, and though Boyle often portrays Ridge haloed by the candle glow of sanctity she also avers to Emanuel Carnevali's remark that Ridge "suffered with the snarl of a lioness… flinging itself madly against the walls of the ugly city… she is one of the most beautiful signs we have of women's emancipation."[18] In short, it is probably true that for all their pretenses to modernity, Josephson, McAlmon, and Loeb were afflicted by a very traditional condescension toward the abilities of women—especially a woman like Ridge who, for all her modernity, clearly viewed the modern world of urban blight, poverty, and the progress of capitalist machine culture in a drastically different light.

In a famous phrase that has curiously come to define his own personal life more than the modern world he sought to describe, T.S. Eliot observed that our world suffered a "dissociation of sensibility," a split between intellect and emotion that the modern poet needed to overcome.[19] For Eliot, as for his fellow expatriate Ezra Pound, the modern world was a shambles. For Pound, this meant that the strong hand of Fascism became a necessary evil in order to restore an imagined golden age of Art and Culture to be appreciated, like all true art, only by the few. For Eliot, in addition to his political and cultural conservatism, it meant embracing an insular version of faith verging on quietism and requiring the renunciation of "strange gods," including the modern world's inevitable tendency to mix communities and races. At the root of Pound's aesthetic elitism is the need to make a religion of Art—"O bright Apollo... / What god, man, or hero / Shall I place a tin wreath upon!"[20] Read in the light of Pound's embrace of Mussolini, these lines from "Hugh Selwyn Mauberly" are prescient in their irony in more ways than the poet first intended. For all his learned recoveries and translations from Homeric Greece, to Troubadour Provence, to T'ang China, Pound's foraging of the cultural past betrays his desire for aesthetic "purity control," an impulse that could not be further from the cultural mélange of the Lower East Side. Eliot's genius also recoils from modernity, and eventually embraces an ideal of ascetic purity. In contrast, Ridge's asceticism points her outward toward the defining "otherness" of her world—the teeming immigrant "ghetto," which is nothing if not an incipient figure for the world we have come to inhabit in the twenty-first century.

Ultimately, for all their brilliant innovations and their drive to "make it new," both Pound and Eliot distrust modernity, and this profound distrust separates them from poets like William Carlos Williams who, as a futurist, embraces an art that forages lovingly among the surfaces and shattered atoms of a world tuned to the rhythms of the machine and guided by its belief in progress. It is for this reason that Williams called *The Wasteland* the great catastrophe, a claim that ironically belies the truth of his rival's insight. There is a dissociation of sensibility in modernism, though beyond the conflicts of intellect and emotion this dissociation strikes at the heart of the West's adherence to the doctrine of perpetual progress fused with and underwritten by capitalist culture. It is this futurist orientation that informed the European editors of *Broom*, Loeb and Josephson, and that dissociated them from Ridge. For Josephson, belief in the Machine Age was tantamount to a faith that could not be renounced without being labeled "retrograde."[21] Though less strident and condescending, Loeb's description of the deterioration of his editorial relationship with Ridge shortly before she quit as American editor of *Broom* characterizes their aesthetic dissociation in precisely these terms:

> *Broom*, in my opinion, should favor writers who appreciated the values in the contemporary scene. This partiality soon brought me into conflict with Lola, who tended to depreciate products of the American capitalist system. To her, capitalism was corrosive, its products corrupt; I felt that capitalism was impersonal, its products magnificent. Since many an untenable religion had in the past inspired glorious artifacts, why shouldn't "money mysticism" do likewise?[22]

Loeb found Ridge maddeningly absolutist in her judgments, though Loeb's seemingly objective account of the rift demonstrates an equally obdurate position. Capitalism is regarded as an impersonal cultural force, not to be judged on its effects on people. The products of capitalism, to use a capital metaphor, are Loeb's only concern. Indeed, he invests them with an "impersonality" as doctrinal as Eliot's claim in "Tradition and the Individual Talent" that all great poetry must be impersonal.[23] Moreover, at the same time as religion is deemed "untenable," and valuable only for its "glorious artifacts," capitalism becomes invested with a spiritual validity of the highest magnitude. Loeb, of course, is recounting a time when many expatriates like himself could absorb the wealth of European life and culture by appealing to the divine economies of their trust funds. That would change after 1929, and the underside of capitalism that Ridge knew and sought to portray became more widely experienced. In any case, it becomes clear from such recollections that Ridge not only distrusted capitalist modernity as vigorously as Eliot and Pound, she also fought to overcome a profound dissociation of sensibility by seeking to fuse together in her own work and the work she championed the incompatible forces of her religious and spiritual idealism with the social and materialist imperatives of her leftist convictions. That fusion, had it been successfully achieved, might have given high modernist poetry another alternative to the futurist secularism of Williams and the cultured pessimism of Pound and Eliot. Instead, Ridge's inability to adequately achieve that synthesis is itself instructive of the internal quarrel that shaped her work as well as the pressures and pitfalls she failed to negotiate in trying to attain the kind of indispensability reached by other poets of her time.

Ridge's first published book of poems, *The Ghetto and Other Poems*, appeared in 1918. It is a volume at once conscious of its desired place in the tradition of American poetry, of its author's drive to innovate upon that tradition, and of its own historical and social moment. The collection begins with a poem of invocation, "To the American People," that echoes Whitman's sweeping democratic vista while at the same time waxing skeptical over the bard's infectious optimism:

> Will you feast with me, American people?
> But what have I that shall seem good to you!
>
> On my board are bitter apples
> And honey served on thorns,
> And in my flagons fluid iron,
> Hot from the crucibles.
>
> How should such fare entice you![24]

Though the poem begins with an invitation, Ridge's conceit of a shared feast quickly devolves into a Blakean plate of oxymorons—bitter apples, honeyed thorns. At first the poem appears emblematic, almost allegorical, but in fact her ironic choice of metaphor instructs the reader to call to mind the brutal world of hunger and poverty that is the other America of breadlines and oppressed workers. With this deft inversion of the reader's expectations, Ridge transforms a song of American innocence into a song of American experience. It is, to use her own words in describing Whitman's poetic revolution, "a grand nihilistic gesture."[25] Just as she envisioned Whitman's poetry assailing "the whole bastille of form and thought" so she frames her own work as an effort to demolish mannerism—what she called in a review of one Georgian anthology the poetry of "a tactful hostess picking her dinner guests."[26] Instead, she would in the manner of her friend and exemplar, Alfred Kreymborg, "deal direct with life," to get out and make a clearing "instead of huddling in mental tenements."[27] Here is Blake's metaphor of "mind-forged manacles" updated to the twentieth century, evocative of a world akin to the stultifying cocktail parties from which Prufrock sought escape.

Real physical tenements, of course, constitute the difficult world about which Ridge chose to write. In a review of one young poet's work she observed that he "lives and writes as one who has lived and suffered with the world's workers."[28] Perhaps nowhere is this judgment more truly applied to her own work than of the long title poem of her first book. "The Ghetto" is a poem in nine numbered sections that depicts in intimate and vivid detail the world of the Jewish immigrants of New York's Lower East Side. Across its sections the poem moves expansively, the way a mural depicts scene after scene until within the wider prospect of the entire structure each individual portrayal gains in significance and intensity. Each section is alternately atmospheric and dramatic, at once offering a catalogue of the world beheld in the teeming streets as well as in the intimacy of domestic relationships. Throughout the poem, Ridge manages to tread the fine line between identifying herself too assertively with these immigrants and merely objectifying them. Nevertheless, an immigrant herself, it is the consciousness of being "other" and nearly anonymous in this dense and vibrant urban landscape that clearly propels her imagination. Here is the poem's opening:

> Cool inaccessible air
> Is floating in velvety blackness shot with steel-blue lights,
> But no breath stirs the heat
> Leaning its ponderous bulk upon the Ghetto
> And most on Hester street...
>
> The heat...
> * * *
> Herring-yellow faces, spotted as with a mold,
> And moist faces of girls
> Like dank white lilies,
> And infant's faces with open parched mouths that suck at
>   the air as at empty teats.[29]

Reading Ridge's evocation of the ghetto through the lens of Eliot's "Prufrock" with its yellow fog and its streets "like an argument of insidious intent," one might be tempted to interpret the scene as one more modernist portrayal of the world's grim meaninglessness. Certainly Ridge has no illusions about the poverty of the world she depicts. However, as the poem proceeds Ridge looks beyond the impotent dismay of Prufrock's fraught consciousness to discover an empathy restorative of human feeling:

Young women pass in groups,
Converging to the forums and meeting halls,
Surging indomitable, slow
Through the gross underbrush of heat.
Their heads are uncovered to the stars,
And they call to the young men and to one another
With a free camaraderie.
Only their eyes are ancient and alone...[30]

What appalled Prufrock, among other things, was the sense of his own decadence and the world's in historical relief of what Pound called "a botched civilization." For all its poverty, severity, and ugliness, Ridge's ghetto is free of decadence. The poor young women are "surging indomitable." The ghetto is no wasteland, and in stark contrast its vision of history is one of continuity and endurance rather than disintegration:

Did they vision—with those eyes darkly clear,
That looked the sun in the face and were not blinded—
Across the centuries
The march of their enduring flesh?
Did they hear—
Under the molten silence
Of the desert like a stopped wheel—
(And the scorpions tick-ticking on the sand...)
The infinite procession of those feet?[31]

"So many, I had not thought death had undone so many," so Eliot invokes Dante in *The Wasteland*, bemoaning the modern Hell of his Unreal City.[32] In contrast, Ridge's city is filled with real people who refuse to succumb to a living death. Where Eliot sees desolation, Ridge envisions life emergent, indomitable, irreducibly various. Likewise, the poet herself refuses the crass anti-Semitism that mars some of Eliot's poems and undermines Pound's authority. Instead, for Ridge, an old scholar has "the wisdom of the Talmud stored away / In his mind's lavender."[33] Here is her portrait of a street trader:

And he—appraising
All who come and go
With his amazing
Sleight-of-mind and glance
And nimble thought
And nature balanced like the scales at nought—
Looks Westward where the trade-lights glow,
And sees his vision rise—
A tape-ruled vision,
Circumscribed in stone—
Some fifty stories to the skies.[34]

Clearly the capitalist spur for profit drives Ridge's trader, though still—contrary to her own political lights—she manages to portray him in the fullness of his humanity. There are no Jews "squatting on the window sill" as we find in "Gerontion." There is, in contrast, a profound awareness of the poet's eye seeking to encounter the other through what Emanuel Levinas would call "an epiphany of the face." In such an epiphany "I and other" are illuminated in a mutually sustaining relationship.

Perhaps most importantly, then, Ridge's ghetto is a social world where—unlike Eliot's solitary ascetic waiting and Pound's glorification of the artist as cultural *Ubermensch*—the longing for transcendence involves communal as well as individual rituals. The old woman who is Ridge's neighbor lights her Sabbath candles, but far from being emblems of her loneliness or symbols of the hermit's lone pursuit of divinity, the candles:

signal
Infinite fine rays
To other windows,
Coupling other lights,
Linking the tenements
Like an endless prayer.[35]

Such communal rituals fill Ridge's poem, and her own patient and generous observance of them at once refuses to objectify the world it encounters and, remarkably, elaborates a promise intimated in Eliot's "Preludes"—the awareness of "some infinitely gentle, infinitely suffering thing" that would bind together the world's fragments, its fractured atoms of solitude. Ridge's perspective here is anything but impersonal in the modernist sense; rather, it is humble before the other she encounters. Indeed, as "The Ghetto" nears its crescendo Ridge denounces "Ego" as the modern world's great ravager with the same vehemence as Pound denouncing "Usury" in *The Cantos*. Strangely enough, for the right-wing Pound and the left-wing Ridge it is the world's subservience to the economic system that breeds social injustice and misfortune, though Ridge's assertion moves beyond materialism to locate the problem in a biological and ultimately spiritual concupiscence to which the world, and in particular capitalism, gives free reign:

Egos out of the shell,
Examining, searching, devouring—
* * *
Egos cawing
Expanding in the mean egg...
* * *
Words, words, words,
Pattering like hail,
Like hail falling without aim...

Egos rampant,
Screaming each other down.
* * *
Egos yearning with the world-old want in their eyes—
* * *
Egos crying out of unkempt deeps
And waving their dreams like flags—[36]

By the end of the poem, Ego with its acquisitive spur has blended into Life that gives birth to "wars, arts, discoveries, rebellions, travails, immolations, cataclysms, hates."[37] Yet, Ridge refuses the temptation to disavow life as a cruel repetition of endlessly repeated and insatiable desires, or another round of madness. For Ridge, even in the black and clotted gutters *"the electric currents of life"* express an indestructible creation:[38]

Strong flux of life,
Like a bitter wine
Out of the bloody stills of the world...
Out of the Passion eternal.[39]

The allusion to Christ's crucifixion in the final lines of "The Ghetto" may at first appear incongruous or, worse, a condescension like Catholic theologian Karl Rahner's notion that other faiths may be forms of "anonymous Christianity." What we find in these lines, however, is a primary instance of Ridge's need as an artist to fuse her own passion for the material plight of the world she encountered with a spiritual ideal. The whole world, and in particular the human struggle to attain meaningful existence, is really the material manifestation of a spiritual desire, a divine urgency that in the poet's achieved perception would confound its defining dualism and redress the demeaning fragmentation of modern life. The poet, like the revolutionary, works in history to reach this ideal; the Passion recurs, and as such Ridge's insight once again finds precedent in Pearse's sacrificial ideal. Similarly, for poetic precedent one thinks of Gerard Manley Hopkins in "As Kingfishers Catch Fire, Dragonflies Draw Flame"—"for Christ plays in ten thousand places / lovely in eyes not his, to the father through the features of men's faces."[40]

In contrast, Objectivism, the indigenous movement in twentieth-century American poetry defined by William Carlos Williams, and later by Charles Olson and George Oppen, eschews any direct appeal to the spiritual in its aesthetic formulation. Objectivism grew, in part at least, out of imagism. Ridge read Pound and Amy Lowell (who became the preeminent practitioner of imagism in the United States). As many of her poems demonstrate, Ridge found imagism a sympathetic technique. She uses it often to create her atmospheric effects in "The Ghetto." More than imagism, objectivism celebrates the materials, the object itself. The most obvious example of the practice is Williams' "The Red Wheelbarrow"—the celebrated "no ideas but in things." At first glance it would seem Ridge's communism would be more sympathetic to the objectivist method, shaped as it is by the materialist refusal of the religious ideal.

Nevertheless, despite her communism, Ridge found pure materialism an insufficient ground both for art and for life. It is for this underlying reason, perhaps, that during her American editorship of *Broom* she rejected poems by Gertrude Stein, since for Stein language itself is material alone, a play of surfaces to be manipulated by the writer. Overruled by Loeb and Josephson in Europe, Ridge quit. On the one hand, Ridge's abrupt severance might be chalked up to jealousy over Stein's accomplishment, though that is highly unlikely—she simply found her work "mostly blah."[41] Or perhaps it was the natural outcome of the slowly degenerating relationship between Ridge and her European editors. That was fueled by Ridge's own editorial convictions. On the other hand, in a letter to Ridge, Loeb asserts that *Broom* had become "an organ with a strongly held point of view."[42] That point of view celebrated modernity and the products of modernity, particularly machine culture. In short, the side of Ridge's sensibility that needed to accommodate a dimension of life greater than life's mere materiality could not abide a point of view that obdurately negated it. The perennial conflict between spirit and flesh, to put it theologically, needed to be surpassed in a synthesis that would not deny the claims of either. For Josephson, Ridge's sensibility was "retrograde" and sentimental.[43] She was at best "an excellent woman who wrote rather dull free verse."[44] One glance at *The Ghetto,* however, reveals an anything but jejune imagination; rather, it showcases Ridge's startling knack for simile and metaphor. In "Flotsam," darkness crouches "like a great cat"; a tired woman sprawls "like a broken beetle" and twigs rattle "like dice."[45] In "Faces":

> A late snow beats
> With cold white fists upon the tenements—
> Hurriedly drawing blinds and shutters,
> Like tall old slatterns
> Pulling aprons about their heads.[46]

In the street, beggars twitch "As though death played / With some ungainly dolls."[47] The Brooklyn Bridge has a "pythoness body." And here is a stunning and arresting figure from "Sons of Belial" in her second book *Sun-Up and Other Poems* where she assumes the identity of a lynch-mob:

> Mad nights when we make ritual
> *(Feet running before the sleuth-light…*
> *And the smell of burnt flesh*
> *By a flame-ringed hut*

In Missouri,
Sweet as on Rome's pyre....)
We make ropes do rigadoons
With copper feet that jig on air.... [48]

Far from being sentimental and retrograde, at its best Ridge's poetry unites what Robert Lowell (alluding to Levi-Straus) would later observe as twentieth-century poetry's tendency to divide itself between "the raw" and "the cooked." The subjects in "Sons of Belial," "The Ghetto" and "Lullaby" (with its living child thrown to the flames by a white woman during a race riot) are as raw as any American poets' in this century. At the same time, her gift for metaphor as well as her tendency to intersperse elevated diction into a poem—the ironic and perversely fanciful "rigadoons" follow "the smell of burnt flesh" in the example above—demonstrates that she can "cook" a poem quite elaborately.

While it is fair to say that in her later work Ridge's poems tend to be somewhat "over-cooked" in their high-flown diction, there are very few such moments in *The Ghetto*. When rhetoric takes over it does so in a way that manifests the poet's urgency to unify her conflicting visions:

Lights go out...
And the great lovers linger in little groups, still passionately
debating,
Or one may walk in silence, listening only to the still
summons of Life—
Life making the great Demand...
Calling its new Christs...
Till tears come, blurring the stars
That grow tender and comforting like the eyes of comrades;
And the moon rolls behind the Battery
Like a word molten out of the mouth of God.[49]

One can see how, in reading these lines, Josephson might make his terse conclusion. They aspire to a high Romanticism worthy of Shelley and, indeed, Ridge won the Shelley Memorial Award in 1935 and 1936. On the other hand, there are passages in Crane shaped to an Elizabethan density that are no less grand in their Romantic musings than Ridge's. The real intent behind such soaring passages in "The Ghetto" is to accommodate a language of biblical and not just Romantic intensity to the circumstances of twentieth-century urban deprivation. Given the subject of the poem, it does not seem a grandiose ambition.

In this aspiration to create a communion between materialism and spirituality in her poetry, Ridge resembles another radical of New York's Lower East Side, Dorothy Day. The lines quoted above—"Life making the great Demand... / Calling its new Christs"—along with the poem's segue to "the eyes of comrades" articulates a sensibility profoundly attuned to that of the great social activist. Founder of *The Catholic Worker* newspaper and its houses of hospitality for the poor, Day (before her conversion) was not only an ardent advocate for social justice, she was also a frequenter of the same artist and literary salons as Ridge. In her biography, *The Long Loneliness*, she recounts joining Kenneth Burke, Malcolm Cowley, and Hart Crane, among others, for the same kind of literary soirées Ridge attended and organized.[50] Like Ridge she was appalled at the prospect of humanity "feeding itself" to the machine.[51] Both had substantial literary aspirations and both shared the same social ideology. Ridge wrote poems in praise of many leftist leaders and agitators, among them Irish American Tom Mooney who spent years in San Quentin after being accused of setting a bomb during a labor rally in San Francisco, and whom Day acknowledges in her biography. Remarkably, in describing the evolution of her own calling, Day uses language profoundly resonant with Ridge's imaginative needs. "I wanted, though I did not know it yet," so Day remarks, "a synthesis. I wanted abundant life. I wanted it for others too..."[52]

In this desire for a synthesis that would satisfy both her religious intuitions and her worldly concerns, Ridge's life and work also anticipate that other extraordinary figure who combined the most intense spiritual urgency with a stark and unflagging attention to the world, Simone Weil. After a year working in factories in the Paris suburbs, Weil wrote her essay "Factory Work," in which she sums up the circumstances of the worker in words that would have rung true to both Day and Ridge. Weil observes:

> The parts circulate with labels bearing their name, material, and degree of elaboration.... One could almost believe they are the persons, and the workers the interchangeable parts.... Things play the role of men, men the role of things. There lies the root of the evil.[53]

Here is Ridge in her poem "Fuel," written sixteen years before:

> What of the silence of the keys
> And silvery hands? The iron sings...
> Though bows lie broken on the strings,
> The fly-wheels turn eternally...
> * * *
> As for the common men apart,
> Who sweat to keep their common breath,
> And have no hour for books or art—
> What dreams have these to hide from death![54]

For Ridge, as for Weil after her, in a world geared toward the fulfillment of abundant life for all, both work and art ought to be spiritual disciplines no less than work and prayer. The difference is that for both of these extraordinary women, as for Day, their St. Benedict's contemplative cell had to be furnished among the tenements and the factories. It is this quest for abundant life, found amidst the welter of life and not in the poet's solitary room nor in the hermit's cell, to which Ridge committed herself in her art.

Indeed, both imaginative poles of Ridge's sensibility—her concern with the material as well as the spiritual life—find their point of intersection in the desire for social justice. Hart Crane's early review of *The Ghetto* seems prescient, then, when he remarks that "the interpretive aspects of her work" appears to be "its most brilliant facet."[55] Though he also affirms the amazing brilliance of her figural imagination ("Over the black bridge / The line of lighted cars / Creeps like a monstrous serpent / Spooring gold…"[56]), he finds her sincerity all the more essential and even cautions her against devolving into "a barren cleverness." While Crane is right to suggest that the interpretive aspects of her work assume prominence over the purely aesthetic pleasure of poetry, it is her impulse to drive home the message—to provide the reader with the moral of the poem as interpreted by the poet—that infuses her poetry as it would evolve of the next twenty years. To that extent, certain poems in *The Ghetto,* like "The Song of Iron," demonstrate Ridge's tendency at times to indulge in rhetorical solutions in seeking to give poetic form to the clash of opposites fueling her imagination:

> Not yet hast Thou sounded
> Thy clangorous music,
> Whose strings are under the mountains…
> Not yet has Thou spoken
> The blooded, implacable Word…

But I hear in the Iron singing—
In the triumphant roaring of the steam and pistons
    pounding—
Thy barbaric exhortation… [57]

As the poem continues, Ridge likens herself to "a cupola" poured for God's use, "a new Mary" into whom the deity might pour "thy molten, world-whelming song." Everything about "The Song of Iron"—the grandiose diction, the syntactical inversions, the hyperbolic imagery—reveals a poet who is striving for some great, definitive utterance. Though the poem intends to waken "Dictators—late Lords of the Iron" to the "blooded, implacable Word," this second coming of Christ as Divine Comrade overwhelms its phrasing and diction. The poet has lapsed into propagandist. The tone is strident, bombastic. Compare the tone of this poem to these lines from "Reveille" in her second book, *Sun-Up and Other Poems*:

As our forefathers stood on the prairies
So let us stand in a ring,
Let us tear up their prisons like grass
And beat them to barricades—
Let us meet the fire of their guns
With a greater fire,
Till the birds shall fly to the mountains
For one safe bough.[58]

The difference in tone between the two poems is extraordinary, though like "The Song of Iron," "Reveille" is also a poem intended to be a call to the workers of the world to rise up in the name of justice against their oppressors, but it accomplishes that intention with a simplicity and immediacy that is enviable. Put simply, regardless of whether one agrees with Ridge's politics, "Reveille" is an infinitely better poem because the poet has beaten back the temptation to assume the mantle of the transfiguring prophet. Despite her passionate convictions, or perhaps because of them, Ridge gradually substitutes the hyperbole of political and religious rhetoric for the genuine quarrel with self by which a poet advances both in the craft of making and in the achievement of a sensibility that continually tests itself against its own convictions. In failing to resist this temptation, Ridge's penchant for "interpretation" leads to an equally strident indulgence in figuralism that Crane warned might transform itself into barren aestheticism. That being said, her strongest work from across the span of her career has not received adequate serious attention for its contributions and historical significance.

One likely reason for Ridge being overlooked by literary history is the time of her death in 1941—the advent of United States involvement in World War II. Though certainly the subject of a poem like "The Ghetto" would have great resonance for the shattering events taking place under Fascism, and particularly against the backdrop of The Holocaust, her leftist views would not have endeared her to the prevailing American milieu. In the 1950s, McCarthyism would have made publishing a poet of Ridge's political cast and urgency impossible. By the 1960s, her work is all but forgotten except as a footnote to the history of American modernist poetry. For the past fifteen years, the main reason there has not been sufficient re-examination of Ridge's work, and absence of discussion of her true importance during the first half of the twentieth century, has been the failure of her estate to produce a *Collected Works* wherein Ridge's lifetime achievement can be framed. Currently, only her first three books are in the public domain. (This impasse, especially with regard to the reissuing of Ridge's last two books, has also impeded research. The purpose of this short selected volume is to go some way toward redressing what is surely a sad literary legacy for Ridge's work. But for unavoidable copyright issues, the present selection would have included two poems from Ridge's earliest, and unpublished, work, *Verses* [written in 1905], "Voice From the Bush" and "At Sun-Down," both written while the poet was still residing in the South Seas, and both prescient of her best later work. This volume would have also included sections from *Firehead* that showcased the best of that book's ambitious verse, as well as selections from *Dance of Fire*, Ridge's last book, including two of its most successful poems, "Stone Face" and "Crucible." Despite the unfortunate circumstances surrounding these absent works, it is important that some introduction to the later poems be provided so that the reader can be encouraged to seek out the remainder of Ridge's body of work, either through library access or the Internet, as well as to encourage the expeditious publication of the *Collected Works*.)

In describing Ridge's later work, Quartermain remarks that her poems "drift toward the abstract and symbolic and toward the mystical and spiritual," though the mystical and spiritual are not new elements in her work but rather constitutive of her imaginative proclivities from the outset.[59] The heavy-handed symbolism and abstraction of her last three books (*Red Flag, Firehead,* and *Dance of Fire*) emerges out of a spiritual urgency present in the best poems of *The Ghetto* and *Sun-Up*, as well as those instances of authentic achievement found in those three later books. At such times, Ridge's spiritual and mystical impulses find embodiment in the materials, in the hard edge of experience. In *Sun-Up*, poems like "Jaguar," "Wall Street at Night," and "East River" muster something of the arresting energy found in Rainer Maria Rilke's *Ding Gedichte*, though in the imagist mode. "Sons of Belial" and "Reveille" are likewise poems that refuse to sacrifice Ridge's vivid realism to pretensions of social and religious prophecy.

The long title sequence "Sun-Up," with its child's voice and swift juxtapositions, anticipates Theodore Roethke's "The Lost Son" in the same way that "The Ghetto" anticipates Galway Kinnell's "The Avenue Bearing the Initial of Christ Into the New World." Moreover, throughout these two books Ridge's poems mark an advance on the portrayal of the voices of women in the poetry of the twentieth century. As such she anticipates the explosion of women's voices in American poetry during the latter half of that century, and in particular the poetry of Muriel Rukeyser finds precedent in Ridge's New York of poor immigrants and workers. She is undoubtedly an important if neglected ancestor for contemporary American women poets, and to American poetry more broadly considered with respect to writers like Philip Levine as well as the plethora of immigrant poetries. Likewise, considered from the standpoint of her own time, she is an insufficiently recognized part of the confluence of politics, culture, and the burgeoning of women's voices at the advent of modernism to the start of World War II.

All this more than suggests that Crane's praise of Ridge's early work was not misplaced, and that Josephson's condescension reflected more his own insecurities as a poet than any particular failure on Ridge's part. At the same time, her work likewise manifests a reaction against the modernist allegiance with the poetics of "art for art's sake" in its insistence on being socially relevant and supportive of The Cause, sometimes at the expense of the poetry. Indeed, there is something of the leftist mural in her work, and murals tend to traffic in panoramas that are emblematic and larger than life. As such, certain poems either become baldly didactic, as in the "Red Flag" sequence that commemorates the Russian Revolution, or highly romanticized, and often both. Of course, there are poems in *Red Flag* like "Mo-ti," "Electrocution," "Kelvin

Barry," and "Street Accident" that retain the fusion between realism and spiritual aspiration that characterizes Ridge at her best. The theological "Death Ray" goes some way toward finding an effective balance between rhetoric and lived experience in its attempt to capture the mystery of incarnation in the ordinary dawn light:

> a stirring at the quick
> of some white palpitating core
> of such intensity as might
> burn up Manhattan like a reed[60]

These lines are memorable and vivid, a fusion of mystical fire and earthly embodiment. Nevertheless, however, the later poems can become increasingly "disembodied" and "curiously abstract"—to use Gregory's apt phrase.[61] It is as though, rather than achieving a dynamic synthesis, the desired marriage of the materialist and the mystic in Ridge had resolved into a series of stylized gestures. Quartermain's evaluation that there is something "retrograde" in her later work holds true, though that should not prompt us to deny her prodigious aspiration in the later poems, nor her successes that manage to skirt the pitfalls of such stylization.[62]

Nowhere is Ridge's penchant for stylization more evident than in the long poem *Firehead* that was to be her magnum opus. Written in response to the Sacco and Vanzetti affair, Ridge's mystical "epic" recounts the crucifixion of Christ from various perspectives, among them that of Judas, the two Marys, Peter, and John. In this, its intention resembles St. Ignatius's method of actively using the imagination to visualize scenes from the life of Christ in order to spur the soul to higher levels of contemplation. There is no direct mention of the trial and execution of the two anarchists, though one suspects that Ridge might have had in mind something of what

Day expresses when she remarks that the sense of solidarity felt at their executions among the poor and the workers made her "gradually understand the doctrine of the Mystical Body of Christ whereby we are members of one another."[63] Indeed, in the opening section of the poem (simply titled "He"), Christ, "the workman's son," is evoked as "the pivot of the world," the central point around which the "lustrous circle" of the universe takes form.[64] The poem also orchestrates images of light, fire, and the moon that had recurred throughout many of the poems of her first three books. In both its attempt to draw together the motifs of her early work and in the sheer audacity of its theme, the poem is stunningly ambitious. By the end of *Firehead,* Ridge goes so far as to place us into Christ's mind as he ascends into heaven. Despite being deemed by Stephen Vincent Benet as a work of genius, and by William Rose Benét "as one of the most remarkable long poems written in… our time,"[65] *Firehead,* in fact, is an epic failure. Quartermain identifies the reason for its failure as "an abstract and incompletely formulated mysticism which makes for prolixity," though the reason for the poem's prolixity lies in the more fundamental failure of Ridge's imagination to accommodate the materiality of human experience within her mystical vision.[66] There are beautifully turned sections of the poem, though they often quickly and uncannily modulate into archaism and bathos. Here, first, are excerpts from Mary Magdallen's dramatic monologue:

> Even when I was a child in Magdala,
> An only one; until my father died
> Imprisoned in his love as in a cell,
> I was a fire secretly burning.[67]

The simplicity and immediacy of the language carries with it the truth of understatement and an authenticity that continues for nearly another forty lines until there is a passage where the monologue might have ended—Magdallen lying naked on the ground in a moment of epiphany feeling "the down-rushing arc / Of heaven making no noise as it broke."[68] Then the poem goes on, its tonal change signaling Ridge's inability to discern the emotionally earned scene from the melodramatic embellishment:

> There sounded a tumultuous music.
> Yet I was weary when I met thee; too many
> And disparate fingers plucked upon my strings
> Vibrating to any touch, until the clear
> Theme was lost.[69]

These lines, with their forced metaphor and their shift to an antiquated mode of address, seem to bespeak the loss of the poem's theme in Ridge's visionary urgency. The bathos intensifies later in the section. "And arrayed in a glamorous fair dress / My soul—for thy continent delight, / For the glance, the scant word of thy praise," so Mary addresses Christ.[70] Here, as in much of *Firehead*, the effort at transfiguration rings false because the transfiguration itself is forced, as though Magdallen had ceased to be a real woman at all but rather a staged oracle for the poet's visionary proclamations. It is as if the poem's individual voices were multiple personalities that modulated without warning from something akin to idiomatic speech to the operatic and hieratic. In turn, *Dance of Fire*, Ridge's final book, is at times even more unabashedly florid in its diction and tone, particularly in the long sonnet sequence "Via Ignis." The twenty-eight poems composing this sequence combine what had become Ridge's hermetic adaptation of light and fire imagery, used traditionally by such mystics as St. John of the Cross in "The Living Flame of Love," with an equally mystical vision of America accomplished with far greater success in Crane's *The Bridge*. There are also echoes of Shelley and Eliot. Not surprisingly, the two most successful poems in the book—"Crucible" and "Stone Face"—commemorate Robinson Jeffers and Tom Mooney, respectively, figures who are not merely figural but whose connection to history, to the natural world, and to human concerns clearly forced Ridge to reassert her allegiance to the core reality of lived experience, even at her most rhetorical:

> The promontory
> Heads are not more lone than he, forever hearing
> The base reef, which the tides, after the torsion, hushed
> with their stroking,
> Mewing as in a tortured sleep, feeling all the rock-saurian
> Body of the coast arching at his touch, made solvent in this
> heat
> Of spirit lambently playing, this audacious
> Fire that would construe to its own image all things...
> even a world.[71]

These lines in praise of Jeffers achieve with far greater dexterity, nobility, and power Ridge's mystical intuition of divinity incarnate in the substances of matter and history—the "dynasty of fire" her later poems sought largely in vain to represent. In describing the limitations of one of her friends and fellow organizers at *The Catholic Worker*, Day remarked that those limitations were caused by the "absorption in the supernatural rather than the natural, in the unseen rather than the seen."[72] Such are the limitations of Ridge's later work when she fails to forge her ideal communion between the opposing materialist and spiritualist poles of her sensibility. It is a synthesis that Day was able to achieve in her life, though she by and large gave up her artistic impulse to achieve that synthesis. At the same time, Ridge's best work, from the beginning to the end of her career, rings consonant with Weil's undeniable truth: "This world into which we are cast does exist; we are truly flesh and blood; we have been thrown out of eternity; and we are indeed obliged to journey painfully through time, minute by and minute out."[73] It was the journey of Lola Ridge's life and work to offer just such a testimony, and her poetic achievement as well as her political commitment may be measured in large part by both her passion and persistence in staying the course.

—Daniel Tobin

Endnotes

1. Quartermain, Peter, "Lola Ridge" in *The Dictionary of Literary Biography*, 54 (Detroit: Gale, 1986), 354.

2. Ibid.

3. Boyle, Kay, & McAlmon, Robert, *Being Geniuses Together* (New York: Doubleday, 1968), 16.

4. Porter, Katherine Anne, *The Never-Ending Wrong* (Boston: Little-Brown, 1977), 23.

5. Gregory, Horace, & Zaturenska, Marina, *A History of American Poetry, 1900–1940* (New York: Gordian Press, 1969), 444.

6. Ibid., 445.

7. Ridge, Lola, *The Ghetto and Other Poems* (New York: B. W. Huebsch, 1918), 101.

8. Ridge, Lola, *Red Flag* (New York: The Viking Press, 1927), 73.

9. Pearse, Padraic, *Plays, Stories, Poems* (Dublin: Talbot Press, 1966), 340.

10. Boyle & McAlmon, *Being Geniuses Together*, 16–17.

11. Ibid., 11.

12. Williams, William Carlos, *The Autobiography of William Carlos Williams* (New York: New Directions, 1951), 135.

13. Boyle & McAlmon, *Being Geniuses Together*, 15.

14. Ibid., 25.

15. Williams, William Carlos, 135.

16. Josephson, Matthew, *Life Among the Surrealists* (New York: Holt, Rinehart, and Winston, 1962), 246.

17. Loeb, Harold, *The Way It Was* (New York: Criterion, 1959), 103.

18. Boyle & McAlmon, *Being Geniuses Together*, 140.

19. Eliot, T.S., *Selected Essays*, edited by Frank Kermode (New York: Harcourt, Brace, Jovanovich, 1975), 64.

20. Pound, Ezra, *Selected Poems* (New York: New Directions, 1957), 63.

21. Josephson, *Life Among the Surrealists*, 246.

22. Loeb, *The Way It Was*, 123.

23. Eliot, *Selected Essays*, 41.

24. Ridge, *The Ghetto and Other Poems*, iii.

25. Ridge, Lola, "Kreymborg's Marionettes," *Dial* 66 (January 11, 1919): 29–31.

26. Ridge, Lola, "The Georgians at Home," *New Republic* 17 (January 11, 1919): 316–317.

27. Ridge, "Kreymborg's Marionettes," *Dial*: 29, 31.

28. Ridge, Lola, "Salt Water," *New Masses* 3 (September 1927): 27.

29. Ridge, *The Ghetto and Other Poems*, 3.

30. Ibid., 4.

31. Ibid., 4–5.

32. Eliot, T.S., *The Complete Poems and Plays, 1909–1950* (New York: Harcourt, Brace and World, 1971), 39.

33. Ridge, *The Ghetto and Other Poems*, 14.

34. Ibid., 15.

35. Ibid., 16–17.

36. Ibid., 19–21.

37. Ibid., 22.

38. Ibid., 25.

39. Ibid., 26.

40. Hopkins, Gerard Manley, *The Poems of Gerard Manley Hopkins*, edited by W. H. Gardiner and N. H. MacKenzie (New York: Oxford University Press, 1967), 90.

41. Josephson, *Life Among the Surrealists*, 231.

42. Loeb, *The Way It Was*, 122.

43. Josephson, *Life Among the Surrealists*, 246.

44. Ibid., 230.

45. Ridge, *The Ghetto and Other Poems*, 33–34.

46. Ibid., 42.

47. Ibid., 43.

48. Ridge, Lola, *Sun-Up and Other Poems* (New York: B. W. Huebsch, 1920), 79.

49. Ridge, *The Ghetto and Other Poems*, 22–23.

50. Day, Dorothy, *The Long Loneliness* (New York: Harper and Row, 1952), 131.

51. Ibid., 171.

52. Ibid., 39.

53. Weil, Simone, *The Simone Weil Reader*, edited by George Panikas (New York: David McKay, 1977), 60.

54. Ridge, *The Ghetto and Other Poems*, 61.

55. Crane, Hart, *The Complete Poems and Selected Letters and Prose of Hart Crane* (New York: Doubleday, 1966), 202.

56. Ridge, *The Ghetto and Other Poems*, 56.

57. Ibid., 49.

58. Ridge, *Sun-Up and Other Poems*, 87.

59. Quartermain, "Lola Ridge" in *The Dictionary of Literary Biography*, 359.

60. Ridge, *Red Flag*, 18.

61. Gregory & Zaturenska, *A History of American Poetry, 1900–1940*, 445.

62. Quatermain, "Lola Ridge" in *The Dictionary of Literary Biography*, 359.

63. Day, *The Long Loneliness*, 147.

64. Ridge, Lola, *Firehead* (New York: Payson and Clarke, 1929), 25, 20, 17.

65. Quartermain, "Lola Ridge" in *The Dictionary of Literary Biography*, 359.

66. Ibid.

67. Ridge, *Firehead*, 113.

68. Ibid., 115.

69. Ibid.

70. Ibid., 122.

71. Ridge, Lola, *Dance of Fire* (New York: Harrison Smith and Robert Haas, 1935), 56.

72. Day, *The Long Loneliness*, 120.

73. Weil, *The Simone Weil Reader*, 69.

THE GHETTO
AND OTHER POEMS

(1918)

The Ghetto

I

Cool inaccessible air
Is floating in velvety blackness shot with steel-blue lights,
But no breath stirs the heat
Leaning its ponderous bulk upon the Ghetto
And most on Hester street...

The heat...
Nosing in the body's overflow,
Like a beast pressing its great steaming belly close,
Covering all avenues of air...

The heat in Hester street,
Heaped like a dray
With the garbage of the world.

Bodies dangle from the fire escapes
Or sprawl over the stoops...
Upturned faces glimmer pallidly—
Herring-yellow faces, spotted as with a mold,
And moist faces of girls
Like dank white lilies,
And infants' faces with open parched mouths that suck at
the air as at empty teats.

Young women pass in groups,
Converging to the forums and meeting halls,
Surging indomitable, slow

Through the gross underbrush of heat.
Their heads are uncovered to the stars,
And they call to the young men and to one another
With a free camaraderie.
Only their eyes are ancient and alone…

The street crawls undulant,
Like a river addled
With its hot tide of flesh
That ever thickens.
Heavy surges of flesh
Break over the pavements,
Clavering like a surf—
Flesh of this abiding
Brood of those ancient mothers who saw the dawn break
over Egypt…
And turned their cakes upon the dry hot stones
And went on
Till the gold of the Egyptians fell down off their arms…
Fasting and athirst…
And yet on…

Did they vision—with those eyes darkly clear,
That looked the sun in the face and were not blinded—
Across the centuries
The march of their enduring flesh?
Did they hear—
Under the molten silence
Of the desert like a stopped wheel—
(And the scorpions tick-ticking on the sand…)
The infinite procession of those feet?

II

I room at Sodos'—in the little green room that was
 Bennie's—
With Sadie
And her old father and her mother,
Who is not so old and wears her own hair.

Old Sodos no longer makes saddles.
He has forgotten how.
He has forgotten most things—even Bennie who stays
 away and sends wine on holidays—
And he does not like Sadie's mother
Who hides God's candles,
Nor Sadie
Whose young pagan breath puts out the light—
That should burn always,
Like Aaron's before the Lord.

Time spins like a crazy dial in his brain,
And night by night
I see the love-gesture of his arm
In its green-greasy coat-sleeve
Circling the Book,
And the candles gleaming starkly
On the blotched-paper whiteness of his face,
Like a miswritten psalm…
Night by night
I hear his lifted praise,
Like a broken whinnying
Before the Lord's shut gate.

Sadie dresses in black.
She has black-wet hair full of cold lights
And a fine-drawn face, too white.
All day the power machines
Drone in her ears…
All day the fine dust flies
Till throats are parched and itch
And the heat—like a kept corpse—
Fouls to the last corner.

Then—when needles move more slowly on the cloth
And sweaty fingers slacken
And hair falls in damp wisps over the eyes—
Sped by some power within,
Sadie quivers like a rod…
A thin black piston flying,
One with her machine.

She—who stabs the piece-work with her bitter eye
And bids the girls: "Slow down—
You'll have him cutting us again!"
She—fiery static atom,
Held in place by the fierce pressure all about—
Speeds up the driven wheels
And biting steel—that twice
Has nipped her to the bone.

Nights, she reads
Those books that have most unset thought,
New-poured and malleable,
To which her thought
Leaps fusing at white heat,
Or spits her fire out in some dim manger of a hall,

Or at a protest meeting on the Square,
Her lit eyes kindling the mob…
Or dances madly at a festival.
Each dawn finds her a little whiter,
Though up and keyed to the long day,
Alert, yet weary… like a bird
That all night long has beat about a light.

The Gentile lover, that she charms and shrews,
Is one more pebble in the pack
For Sadie's mother,
Who greets him with her narrowed eyes
That hold some welcome back.
"What's to be done?" she'll say,
"When Sadie wants she takes…
Better than Bennie with his Christian woman…
A man is not so like,
If they should fight,
To call her Jew…"

Yet when she lies in bed
And the soft babble of their talk comes to her
And the silences…
I know she never sleeps
Till the keen draught blowing up the empty hall
Edges through her transom
And she hears his foot on the first stairs.

Sarah and Anna live on the floor above.
Sarah is swarthy and ill-dressed.
Life for her has no ritual.
She would break an ideal like an egg for the winged thing at
the core.

Her mind is hard and brilliant and cutting like an acetylene
torch.
If any impurities drift there, they must be burnt up as in a
clear flame.
It is droll that she should work in a pants factory.
—Yet where else... tousled and collar awry at her olive throat.
Besides her hands are unkempt.
With English... and everything... there is so little time.
She reads without bias—
Doubting clamorously—
Psychology, plays, science, philosophies—
Those giant flowers that have bloomed and withered,
scattering their seed...
—And out of this young forcing soil what growth may
come—what amazing blossomings.

Anna is different.
One is always aware of Anna, and the young men turn their
heads to look at her.
She has the appeal of a folk-song
And her cheap clothes are always in rhythm.
When the strike was on she gave half her pay.
She would give anything—save the praise that is hers
And the love of her lyric body.

But Sarah's desire covets nothing apart.
She would share all things...
Even her lover.

III

The sturdy Ghetto children
March by the parade,
Waving their toy flags,
Prancing to the bugles—
Lusty, unafraid...
Shaking little fire sticks
At the night—
The old blinking night—
Swerving out of the way,
Wrapped in her darkness like a shawl.

But a small girl
Cowers apart.
Her braided head,
Shiny as a black-bird's
In the gleam of the torch-light,
Is poised as for flight.
Her eyes have the glow
Of darkened lights.

She stammers in Yiddish,
But I do not understand,
And there flits across her face
A shadow
As of a drawn blind.
I give her an orange,
Large and golden,
And she looks at it blankly.
I take her little cold hand and try to draw her to me,
But she is stiff...
Like a doll...

Suddenly she darts through the crowd
Like a little white panic
Blown along the night—
Away from the terror of oncoming feet...
And drums rattling like curses in red roaring mouths...
And torches spluttering silver fire
And lights that nose out hiding places...
To the night—
Squatting like a hunchback
Under the curved stoop—
The old mammy-night
That has outlived beauty and knows the ways of fear—
The night—wide-opening crooked and comforting arms,
Hiding her as in a voluminous skirt.

The sturdy Ghetto children
March by the parade,
Waving their toy flags,
Prancing to the bugles,
Lusty, unafraid.
But I see a white frock
And eyes like hooded lights
Out of the shadow of pogroms
Watching... watching...

IV

Calicoes and furs,
Pocket-books and scarfs,
Razor strops and knives
(Patterns in check...)

Olive hands and russet head,
Pickles red and coppery.
Green pickles, brown pickles,
(Patterns in tapestry...)

Coral beads, blue beads,
Beads of pearl and amber,
Gewgaws, beauty pins—
Bijoutry for chits—
Darting rays of violet,
Amethyst and jade...
All the colors out to play,
Jumbled iridescently...
(Patterns in stained glass
Shivered into bits!)

Nooses of gay ribbon
Tugging at one's sleeve,
Dainty little garters
Hanging out their sign...
Here a pout of frilly things—
There a sonsy feather...
(White beards, black beards
Like knots in the weave...)

And ah, the little babies—
Shiny black-eyed babies—
(Half a million pink toes
Wriggling altogether.)
Baskets full of babies
Like grapes on a vine.

Mothers waddling in and out,
Making all things right—
Picking up the slipped threads
In Grand street at night—
Grand street like a great bazaar,
Crowded like a float,
Bulging like a crazy quilt
Stretched on a line.

But nearer seen
This litter of the East
Takes on a garbled majesty.

The herded stalls
In dissolute array...
The glitter and the jumbled finery
And strangely juxtaposed
Cans, paper, rags
And colors decomposing,
Faded like old hair,
With flashes of barbaric hues
And eyes of mystery...
Flung
Like an ancient tapestry of motley weave
Upon the open wall of this new land.

Here, a tawny-headed girl...
Lemons in a greenish broth
And a huge earthen bowl
By a bronzed merchant
With a tall black lamb's wool cap upon his head...
He has no glance for her.
His thrifty eyes

Bend—glittering, intent
Their hoarded looks
Upon his merchandise,
As though it were some splendid cloth
Or sumptuous raiment
Stitched in gold and red...

He seldom talks
Save of the goods he spreads—
The meager cotton with its dismal flower—
But with his skinny hands
That hover like two hawks
Above some luscious meat,
He fingers lovingly each calico,
As though it were a gorgeous shawl,
Or costly vesture
Wrought in silken thread,
Or strange bright carpet
Made for sandaled feet...

Here an old grey scholar stands.
His brooding eyes—
That hold long vistas without end
Of caravans and trees and roads,
And cities dwindling in remembrance—
Bend mostly on his tapes and thread.

What if they tweak his beard—
These raw young seed of Israel
Who have no backward vision in their eyes—
And mock him as he sways
Above the sunken arches of his feet—
They find no peg to hang their taunts upon.

His soul is like a rock
That bears a front worn smooth
By the coarse fiction of the sea,
And, unperturbed, he keeps his bitter peace.

What if a rigid arm and stuffed blue shape,
Backed by a nickel star
Does prod him on,
Taking his proud patience for humility...
All gutters are as one
To that old race that has been thrust
From off the curbstones of the world...
And he smiles with the pale irony
Of one who holds
The wisdom of the Talmud stored away
In his mind's lavender.

But this young trader,
Born to trade as to a caul,
Peddles the notions of the hour.
The gestures of the craft are his
And all the lore
As when to hold, withdraw, persuade, advance...
And be it gum or flags,
Or clean-all or the newest thing in tags,
Demand goes to him as the bee to flower.
And he—appraising
All who come and go
With his amazing
Sleight-of-mind and glance
And nimble thought
And nature balanced like the scales at nought—
Looks Westward where the trade-lights glow,

And sees his vision rise—
A tape-ruled vision,
Circumscribed in stone—
Some fifty stories to the skies.

V

As I sit in my little fifth-floor room—
Bare,
Save for bed and chair,
And coppery stains
Left by seeping rains
On the low ceiling
And green plaster walls,
Where when night falls
Golden lady-bugs
Come out of their holes,
And roaches, sepia-brown, consort...
I hear bells pealing
Out of the gray church at Rutgers street,
Holding its high-flung cross above the Ghetto,
And, one floor down across the court,
The parrot screaming:
Vorwärts... Vorwärts...

The parrot frowsy-white,
Everlastingly swinging
On its iron bar.

A little old woman,
With a wig of smooth black hair
Gummed about her shrunken brows,

Comes sometimes on the fire escape.
An old stooped mother,
The left shoulder low
With that uneven droopiness that women know
Who have suckled many young...
Yet I have seen no other than the parrot there.

I watch her mornings as she shakes her rugs
Feebly, with futile reach
And fingers without clutch.
Her thews are slack
And curved the ruined back
And flesh empurpled like old meat,
Yet each conspires
To feed those guttering fires
With which her eyes are quick.

On Friday nights
Her candles signal
Infinite fine rays
To other windows,
Coupling other lights,
Linking the tenements
Like an endless prayer.

She seems less lonely than the bird
That day by day about the dismal house
Screams out his frenzied word...
That night by night—
If a dog yelps
Or a cat yawls
Or a sick child whines,

Or a door screaks on its hinges,
Or a man and woman fight—
Sends his cry above the huddled roofs:
Vorwärts... Vorwärts...

VI

In this dingy café
The old men sit muffled in woolens.
Everything is faded, shabby, colorless, old...
The chairs, loose-jointed,
Creaking like old bones—
The tables, the waiters, the walls,
Whose mottled plaster
Blends in one tone with the old flesh.

Young life and young thought are alike barred,
And no unheralded noises jolt old nerves,
And old wheezy breaths
Pass around old thoughts, dry as snuff,
And there is no divergence and no friction
Because life is flattened and ground as by many mills.

And it is here the Committee—
Sweet-breathed and smooth of skin
And supple of spine and knee,
With shining unpouched eyes
And the blood, high-powered,
Leaping in flexible arteries—
The insolent, young, enthusiastic, undiscriminating
    Committee,

Who would placard tombstones
And scatter leaflets even in graves,
Comes trampling with sacrilegious feet!

The old men turn stiffly,
Mumbling to each other.
They are gentle and torpid and busy with eating.
But one lifts a face of clayish pallor,
There is a dull fury in his eyes, like little rusty grates.
He rises slowly,
Trembling in his many swathings like an awakened mummy,
Ridiculous yet terrible.
—And the Committee flings him a waste glance,
Dropping a leaflet by his plate.

A lone fire flickers in the dusty eyes.
The lips chant inaudibly.
The warped shrunken body straightens like a tree.
And he curses...
With uplifted arms and perished fingers,
Claw-like, clutching...
So centuries ago
The old men cursed Acosta,
When they, prophetic, heard upon their sepulchres
Those feet that may not halt nor turn aside for ancient
things.

VII

Here in this room, bare like a barn,
Egos gesture one to the other—
Naked, unformed, unwinged

Egos out of the shell,
Examining, searching, devouring—
Avid alike for the flower or the dung...
(Having no dainty antennæ for the touch and withdrawal—
Only the open maw...)

Egos cawing,
Expanding in the mean egg...
Little squat tailors with unkempt faces,
Pale as lard,
Fur-makers, factory-hands, shop-workers,
News-boys with battling eyes
And bodies yet vibrant with the momentum of long runs,
Here and there a woman...

Words, words, words,
Pattering like hail,
Like hail falling without aim...
Egos rampant,
Screaming each other down.

One motions perpetually,
Waving arms like overgrowths.
He has burning eyes and a cough
And a thin voice piping
Like a flute among trombones.

One, red-bearded, rearing
A welter of maimed face bashed in from some old wound,
Garbles Max Stirner.
His words knock each other like little wooden blocks.
No one heeds him,
And a lank boy with hair over his eyes

Pounds upon the table,
—He is chairman.

Egos yet in the primer,
Hearing world-voices
Chanting grand arias…
Majors resonant,
Stunning with sound…
Baffling minors
Half-heard like rain on pools…
Majestic discordances
Greater than harmonies…
—Gleaning out of it all
Passion, bewilderment, pain…

Egos yearning with the world-old want in their eyes—
Hurt hot eyes that do not sleep enough…
Striving with infinite effort,
Frustrate yet ever pursuing
The great white Liberty,
Trailing her dissolving glory over each hard-won barricade—
Only to fade anew…

Egos crying out of unkempt deeps
And waving their dreams like flags—
Multi-colored dreams,
Winged and glorious…

A gas jet throws a stunted flame,
Vaguely illumining the groping faces.
And through the uncurtained window
Falls the waste light of stars,
As cold as wise men's eyes…

Indifferent great stars,
Fortuitously glancing
At the secret meeting in this shut-in room,
Bare as a manger.

VIII

Lights go out
And the stark trunks of the factories
Melt into the drawn darkness,
Sheathing like a seamless garment.

And mothers take home their babies,
Waxen and delicately curled,
Like little potted flowers closed under the stars.

Lights go out
And the young men shut their eyes,
But life turns in them...
Life in the cramped ova
Tearing and rending asunder its living cells...
Wars, arts, discoveries, rebellions, travails, immolations,
cataclysms, hates...
Pent in the shut flesh.
And the young men twist on their beds in languor and
dizziness unsupportable...
Their eyes—heavy and dimmed
With dust of long oblivions in the gray pulp behind—
Staring as through a choked glass.
And they gaze at the moon—throwing off a faint heat—
The moon, blond and burning, creeping to their cots
Softly, as on naked feet...

Lolling on the coverlet… like a woman offering her white
body.

Nude glory of the moon!
That leaps like an athlete on the bosoms of the young girls
stripped of their linens;
Stroking their breasts that are smooth and cool as mother-
of-pearl
Till the nipples tingle and burn as though little lips plucked
at them.
They shudder and grow faint.
And their ears are filled as with a delirious rhapsody,
That Life, like a drunken player,
Strikes out of their clear white bodies
As out of ivory keys.

Lights go out…
And the great lovers linger in little groups, still passionately
debating,
Or one may walk in silence, listening only to the still
summons of Life—
Life making the great Demand…
Calling its new Christs…
Till tears come, blurring the stars
That grow tender and comforting like the eyes of comrades;
And the moon rolls behind the Battery
Like a word molten out of the mouth of God.

Lights go out…
And colors rush together,
Fusing and floating away…
Pale worn gold like the settings of old jewels…
Mauves, exquisite, tremulous, and luminous purples

And burning spires in aureoles of light
Like shimmering auras.

They are covering up the pushcarts ..
Now all have gone save an old man with mirrors—
Little oval mirrors like tiny pools.
He shuffles up a darkened street
And the moon burnishes his mirrors till they shine like
        phosphorus…
The moon like a skull,
Staring out of eyeless sockets at the old men trundling
        home the pushcarts.

IX

A sallow dawn is in the sky
As I enter my little green room.
Sadie's light is still burning…
Without, the frail moon
Worn to a silvery tissue,
Throws a faint glamour on the roofs,
And down the shadowy spires
Lights tip-toe out…
Softly as when lovers close street doors.

Out of the Battery
A little wind
Stirs idly—as an arm
Trails over a boat's side in dalliance—
Rippling the smooth dead surface of the heat,
And Hester street,
Like a forlorn woman over-born

By many babies at her teats,
Turns on her trampled bed to meet the day.

LIFE!

Startling, vigorous life,
That squirms under my touch,
And baffles me when I try to examine it,
Or hurls me back without apology.
Leaving my ego ruffled and preening itself.

Life,
Articulate, shrill,
Screaming in provocative assertion,
Or out of the black and clotted gutters,
Piping in silvery thin
Sweet staccato
Of children's laughter,
Or clinging over the pushcarts
Like a litter of tiny bells
Or the jingle of silver coins,
Perpetually changing hands,
Or like the Jordan somberly
Swirling in tumultuous uncharted tides,
Surface-calm.

Electric currents of life,
Throwing off thoughts like sparks,
Glittering, disappearing,
Making unknown circuits,
Or out of spent particles stirring
Feeble contortions in old faiths
Passing before the new.

Long nights argued away
In meeting halls
Back of interminable stairways—
In Roumanian wine-shops
And little Russian tea-rooms…

Feet echoing through deserted streets
In the soft darkness before dawn…
Brows aching, throbbing, burning—
Life leaping in the shaken flesh
Like flame at an asbestos curtain,

Life—
Pent, overflowing
Stoops and façades,
Jostling, pushing, contriving,
Seething as in a great vat …

Bartering, changing, extorting,
Dreaming, debating, aspiring,
Astounding, indestructible
Life of the Ghetto…

Strong flux of life,
Like a bitter wine
Out of the bloody stills of the world…
Out of the Passion eternal.

Flotsam

Crass rays streaming from the vestibules;
Cafés glittering like jeweled teeth;
High-flung signs
Blinking yellow phosphorescent eyes;
Girls in black
Circling monotonously
About the orange lights…

Nothing to guess at…
Save the darkness above
Crouching like a great cat.

In the dim-lit square,
Where dishevelled trees
Tustle with the wind—the wind like a scythe
Mowing their last leaves—
Arcs shimmering through a greenish haze—
Pale oval arcs
Like ailing virgins,
Each out of a halo circumscribed,
Pallidly staring…

Figures drift upon the benches
With no more rustle than a dropped leaf settling—
Slovenly figures like untied parcels,
And papers wrapped about their knees
Huddled one to the other,
Cringing to the wind—
The sided wind,
Leaving no breach untried…

So many and all so still…
The fountain slobbering its stone basin
Is louder than They—
Flotsam of the five oceans
Here on this raft of the world.

This old man's head
Has found a woman's shoulder.
The wind juggles with her shawl
That flaps about them like a sail,
And splashes her red faded hair
Over the salt stubble of his chin.
A light foam is on his lips,
As though dreams surged in him
Breaking and ebbing away…
And the bare boughs shuffle above him
And the twigs rattle like dice…

She—diffused like a broken beetle—
Sprawls without grace,
Her face gray as asphalt,
Her jaws sagging as on loosened hinges…
Shadows ply about her mouth—
Nimble shadows out of the jigging tree,
That dances above her its dance of dry bones.

II

A uniformed front,
Paunched;
A glance like a blow,
The swing of an arm,

Verved, vigorous;
Boot-heels clanking
In metallic rhythm;
The blows of a baton,
Quick, staccato...

—There is a rustling along the benches
As of dried leaves raked over...
And the old man lifts a shaking palsied hand,
Tucking the displaced paper about his knees.

Colder...
And a frost under foot,
Acid, corroding,
Eating through worn bootsoles.

Drab forms blur into greenish vapor.
Through boughs like cross-bones,
Pale arcs flare and shiver
Like lilies in a wind.

High over Broadway
A far-flung sign
Glitters in indigo darkness
And spurts again rhythmically,
Spraying great drops
Red as a hemorrhage.

Faces

A late snow beats
With cold white fists upon the tenements—
Hurriedly drawing blinds and shutters,
Like tall old slatterns
Pulling aprons about their heads.

Lights slanting out of Mott Street
Gibber out,
Or dribble through bar-room slits,
Anonymous shapes
Conniving behind shuttered panes
Caper and disappear…
Where the Bowery
Is throbbing like a fistula
Back of her ice-scabbed fronts.

Livid faces
Glimmer in furtive doorways,
Or spill out of the black pockets of alleys,
Smears of faces like muddied beads,
Making a ghastly rosary
The night mumbles over
And the snow with its devilish and silken whisper…
Patrolling arcs
Blowing shrill blasts over the Bread Line
Stalk them as they pass,
Silent as though accouched of the darkness,
And the wind noses among them,
                    Like a skunk
That roots about the heart…

Colder:
And the Elevated slams upon the silence
Like a ponderous door.
Then all is still again,
Save for the wind fumbling over
The emptily swaying faces—
The wind rummaging
Like an old Jew...

Faces in glimmering rows...
(No sign of the abject life—
Not even a blasphemy...)
But the spindle legs keep time
To a limping rhythm,
And the shadows twitch upon the snow
Convulsively—
As though death played
With some ungainly dolls.

Débris

I love those spirits
That men stand off and point at,
Or shudder and hood up their souls—
Those ruined ones,
Where Liberty has lodged an hour
And passed like flame,
Bursting asunder the too small house.

Frank Little at Calvary

I

He walked under the shadow of the Hill
Where men are fed into the fires
And walled apart…
Unarmed and alone,
He summoned his mates from the pit's mouth
Where tools rested on the floors
And great cranes swung
Unemptied, on the iron girders.
And they, who were the Lords of the Hill,
Were seized with a great fear,
When they heard out of the silence of wheels
The answer ringing
In endless reverberations
Under the mountain…

So they covered up their faces
And crept upon him as he slept…
Out of eye-holes in black cloth
They looked upon him who had flung
Between them and their ancient prey
The frail barricade of his life…
And when night—that has connived at so much—
Was heavy with the unborn day,
They haled him from his bed…

Who may know of that wild ride?
Only the bleak Hill—

The red Hill, vigilant,
Like a blood-shot eye
In the black mask of night—
Dared watch them as they raced
By each blind-folded street
Godiva might have ridden down...
But when they stopped beside the Place,
I know he turned his face
Wistfully to the accessory night...

And when he saw—against the sky,
Sagged like a silken net
Under its load of stars—
The black bridge poised
Like a gigantic spider motionless...
I know there was a silence in his heart,
As of a frozen sea,
Where some half lifted arm, mid-way
Wavers, and drops heavily...

I know he waved to life,
And that life signaled back, transcending space,
To each high-powered sense,
So that he missed no gesture of the wind
Drawing the shut leaves close...
So that he saw the light on comrades' faces
Of camp fires out of sight...
And the savor of meat and bread
Blew in his nostrils... and the breath
Of unrailed spaces
Where shut wild clover smelled as sweet
As a virgin in her bed.

I know he looked once at America,
Quiescent, with her great flanks on the globe,
And once at the skies whirling above him...
Then all that he had spoken against
And struck against and thrust against
Over the frail barricade of his life
Rushed between him and the stars...

II

Life thunders on...
Over the black bridge
The line of lighted cars
Creeps like a monstrous serpent
Spooring gold...

Watchman, what of the track?

Night... silence... stars...
All's Well!

III

Light...
(Breaking mists...
Hills gliding like hands out of a slipping hold...)
Light over the pit mouths,
Streaming in tenuous rays down the black gullets of the
Hill...
(The copper, insensate, sleeping in the buried lode.)

Light...
Forcing the clogged windows of arsenals...
Probing with long sentient fingers in the copper chips...
Gleaming metallic and cold
In numberless slivers of steel...
Light over the trestles and the iron clips
Of the black bridge—poised like a gigantic spider
        motionless—
Sweet inquisition of light, like a child's wonder...
Intrusive, innocently staring light
That nothing appals...

Light in the slow fumbling summer leaves,
Cooing and calling
All winged and avid things
Waking the early flies, keen to the scent...
Green-jeweled iridescent flies
Unerringly steering—
Swarming over the blackened lips,
The young day sprays with indiscriminate gold...

Watchman, what of the Hill?

Wheels turn;
The laden cars
Go rumbling to the mill,
And Labor walks beside the mules...
All's Well with the Hill!

The Legion of Iron

They pass through the great iron gates—
Men with eyes gravely discerning,
Skilled to appraise the tunnage of cranes
Or split an inch into thousandths—
Men tempered by fire as the ore is
And planned to resistance
Like steel that has cooled in the trough;
Silent of purpose, inflexible, set to fulfilment—
To conquer, withstand, overthrow…
Men mannered to large undertakings,
Knowing force as a brother
And power as something to play with,
Seeing blood as a slip of the iron,
To be wiped from the tools
Lest they rust.

But what if they stood aside?
Who hold the earth so careless in the crook of their arms?

What of the flamboyant cities
And the lights guttering out like candles in a wind…
And the armies halted…
And the train mid-way on the mountain
And idle men chaffing across the trenches…
And the cursing and lamentation
And the clamor for grain shut in the mills of the world?
What if they stayed apart,
Inscrutably smiling,
Leaving the ground encumbered with dead wire

And the sea to row-boats
And the lands marooned—
Till Time should like a paralytic sit,
A mildewed hulk above the nations squatting?

Fuel

What of the silence of the keys
And silvery hands? The iron sings…
Though bows lie broken on the strings,
The fly-wheels turn eternally…

Bring fuel—drive the fires high…
Throw all this artist-lumber in
And foolish dreams of making things…
(Ten million men are called to die.)

As for the common men apart,
Who sweat to keep their common breath,
And have no hour for books or art—
What dreams have these to hide from death!

"The Everlasting Return"

It is dark... so dark, I remember the sun on Chios...
It is still... so still, I hear the beat of our paddles on the Ægean...

Ten times we had watched the moon
Rise like a thin white virgin out of the waters
And round into a full maternity...
For thrice ten moons we had touched no flesh
Save the man flesh on either hand
That was black and bitter and salt
    and scaled by the sea.

The Athenian boy sat on my left...
His hair was yellow as corn steeped in wine...
And on my right was Phildar the Carthaginian,
Grinning Phildar
With his mouth pulled taut as by reins
    from his black gapped teeth.
Many a whip had coiled about him
And his shoulders were rutted deep
    as wet ground under chariot wheels,
And his skin was red and tough
    as a bull's hide cured in the sun.
He did not sing like the other slaves,
But when a big wind came up he screamed with it.
And always he looked out to sea,
Save when he tore at his fish ends
Or spat across me at the Greek boy,
    whose mouth was red and apart like an opened fruit.

We had rowed from dawn and the green valley
hard at our stern.
She was green and squat and skulked close to the sea.
All day the *tish* of their paddles had tickled our ears,
And when night came on
And little naked stars dabbled in the water
And half the crouching moon
Slid over the silver belly of the sea
thick-scaled with light,
We heard them singing at their oars...
We who had no breath for song.

There was no sound in our boat
Save the clingle of wrist chains
And the sobbing of the young Greek.
I cursed him that his hair blew in my mouth,
tasting salt of the sea...
I cursed him that his oar kept ill time...
When he looked at me I cursed him again,
That his eyes were soft as a woman's.

How long... since their last shell gouged our batteries?
How long... since we rose at aim with a sleuth moon astern?
(It was the damned green moon that nosed us out...
The moon that flushed our periscope till it shone like a silver
flame...)

They loosed each man's right hand
As the galley spent on our decks...
And amazed and bloodied we reared half up
And fought askew with the left hand shackled...
But a zigzag fire leapt in our sockets
And knotted our thews like string...

Our thews grown stiff as a crooked spine
 that would not straighten...

How long... since our gauges fell
And the sea shoved us under?
It is dark... so dark...
Darkness presses hairy-hot
Where three make crowded company...
And the rank steel smells...
It is still... so still...
I seem to hear the wind
On the dimpled face of the water
 fathoms above...

It was still... so still... we three that were left alive
Stared in each other's faces...
But three make better company at one man's bread...
And our hate grew sharp and bright
 as the moon's edge in the water.
One grinned with his mouth awry
 from the long gapped teeth...
And one shivered and whined like a gull
 as the waves pawed us over...
But one struck with his hate in his hand...

After that I remember
Only the dead men's oars that flapped in the sea...
The dead men's oars that rattled and clicked
 like idiots' tongues.

It is still... so still, with the jargon of engines quiet.
We three awaiting the crunch of the sea
Reach our hands in the dark and touch each other's faces...

We three sheathing hate in our hearts…
But when hate shall have made its circuit,
Our bones will be loving company
Here in the sea's den…
And one whimpers and cries on his God
And one sits sullenly
But both draw away from me…
For I am the pyre their memories burn on…
Like black flames leaping
Our fiery gestures light the walled-in
darkness of the sea…
The sea that kneels above us…
And makes no sign.

Palestine

Old plant of Asia—
Mutilated vine
Holding earth's leaping sap
In every stem and shoot
That lopped off, sprouts again—
Why should you seek a plateau walled about,
Whose garden is the world?

To the Others

I see you, refulgent ones,
Burning so steadily
Like big white arc lights...
There are so many of you.
I like to watch you weaving—
Altogether and with precision
Each his ray—
Your tracery of light,
Making a shining way about America.

I note your infinite reactions—
In glassware
And sequin
And puddles
And bits of jet—
And here and there a diamond...

But you do not yet see me,
Who am a torch blown along the wind,
Flickering to a spark
But never out.

The Fiddler

In a little Hungarian café
Men and women are drinking
Yellow wine in tall goblets.

Through the milky haze of the smoke,
The fiddler, under-sized, blond,
Leans to his violin
As to the breast of a woman.
Red hair kindles to fire
On the black of his coat-sleeve,
Where his white thin hand
Trembles and dives,
Like a sliver of moonlight,
When wind has broken the water.

Brooklyn Bridge

Pythoness body—arching
Over the night like an ecstasy—
I feel your coils tightening…
And the world's lessening breath.

The Edge

I thought to die that night in the solitude where they would
never find me…
But there was time…
And I lay quietly on the drawn knees of the mountain,
staring into the abyss…
I do not know how long…
I could not count the hours, they ran so fast
Like little bare-foot urchins—shaking my hands away…
But I remember
Somewhere water trickled like a thin severed vein…
And a wind came out of the grass,
Touching me gently, tentatively, like a paw.

As the night grew
The gray cloud that had covered the sky like sackcloth
Fell in ashen folds about the hills,
Like hooded virgins, pulling their cloaks about them…
There must have been a spent moon,
For the Tall One's veil held a shimmer of silver…

That too I remember…
And the tenderly rocking mountain
Silence
And beating stars…
Dawn
Lay like a waxen hand upon the world,
And folded hills
Broke into a sudden wonder of peaks, stemming clear and
cold,

Till the Tall One bloomed like a lily,
Flecked with sun,
Fine as a golden pollen—
It seemed a wind might blow it from the snow.

I smelled the raw sweet essences of things,
And heard spiders in the leaves
And ticking of little feet,
As tiny creatures came out of their doors
To see God pouring light into his star…

…It seemed life held
No future and no past but this…

And I too got up stiffly from the earth,
And held my heart up like a cup…

SUN-UP
AND OTHER POEMS

(1920)

from Sun-Up

Sun-Up

(Shadows over a cradle…
fire-light craning…
A hand
throws something in the fire
and a smaller hand
runs into the flame and out again,
singed and empty…
Shadows
settling over a cradle…
two hands
and a fire.)

I
Celia

Cherry, cherry,
glowing on the hearth,
bright red cherry…
When you try to pick up cherry
Celia's shriek
sticks in you like a pin.

: :

When God throws hailstones
you cuddle in Celia's shawl
and press your feet on her belly
high up like a stool.
When Celia makes umbrella of her hand.
Rain falls through
big pink spokes of her fingers.
When wind blows Celia's gown up off her legs
she runs under pillars of the bank—
great round pillars of the bank
have on white stockings too.

: :

Celia says my father
will bring me a golden bowl.
When I think of my father
I cannot see him
for the big yellow bowl
like the moon with two handles
he carries in front of him.

: :

Grandpa, grandpa...
(Light all about you...
ginger... pouring out of green jars...)
You don't believe he has gone away and left his great coat...
so you pretend... you see his face up in the ceiling.
When you clap your hands and cry, grandpa, grandpa,
    grandpa ,
Celia crosses herself.

: :

It isn't a dream...
It comes again and again...
You hear ivy crying on steeples
the flames haven't caught yet
and images screaming
when they see red light on the lilies
on the stained glass window of St. Joseph.
The girl with the black eyes holds you tight,
and you run... and run
past the wild, wild towers...
and trees in the gardens tugging at their feet
and little frightened dolls
shut up in the shops
crying... and crying... because no one stops...
you spin like a penny thrown out in the street.
Then the man clutches her by the hair...
He always clutches her by the hair...
His eyes stick out like spears.
You see her pulled-back face
and her black, black eyes
lit up by the glare...
Then everything goes out.

Please God, don't let me dream any more
of the girl with the black, black eyes.

: :

Celia's shadow rocks and rocks...
and mama's eyes stare out of the pillow
as though she had gone away
and the night had come in her place
as it comes in empty rooms...
you can't bear it—
the night threshing about
and lashing its tails on its sides
as bold as a wolf that isn't afraid—
and you scream at her face, that is white as a stone on a grave
and pull it around to the light,
till the night draws backward... the night that walks alone
and goes away without end.
Mama says, I am cold, Betty, and shivers.
Celia tucks the quilt about her feet,
but I run for my little red cloak
because red is hot like fire.

: :

I wish Celia
could see the sea climb up on the sky
and slide off again...
... Celia saying
I'd beg the world with you...
Celia... holding on to the cab...
hands wrenched away...
wind in the masts... like Celia crying...
Celia never minded if you slapped her
when the comb made your hairs ache,

but though you rub your cheek against mama's hand
she has not said darling since…
Now I will slap her again…
I will bite her hand till it bleeds.

It is cool by the port hole.
The wet rags of the wind
flap in your face.

III
Mama

Mama's face
is smooth and pale as tea-rose leaves.
That ivory oval of aunt Gem
you sucked the miniature off
had black black hair like mama.

: :

Pit-it-ty-pat,
Mama walks so fast,
street lamps jig
without bending a leg…
lights in the windows
play twinkling tunes
on crimson and blue
bottles like bubbles
big as balloons…
Faster and faster…
and pink light spurts
over cakes doing polkas
in little white shirts,
with cake-princesses
in flounced white skirts.
Pit-pat—
mama walks slower…
slower and… slower…
Eyes… lamps… stars…
acres and acres of stars…
bells… and sleepily
flapping feet…
You're glad mama walks slow.

It's nice to be carried along
up high near the stars
that look at you with a grave, great look.

: :

Every night
mama sings you to sleep.
When she sings, *O for the light of thine eyes Dolores,*
there's a castle on a cliff
and the sea roars like lions.
It leaps at the castle
and the cliff knocks it down
but always the sea
shakes its flattened head
and gets up again.
The castle has no roof
so the rain spins silvery webs in it,
and Dolores' face
floats dim and beautiful
the way flowers do when they are drowned.
Step by white step
she goes up the castle stairs,
but the stair goes up into the sky
and the sky keeps going up too,
so none of them ever get there.

When mama sings *Ba ba black sheep,*
the stars seem to shine through her voice
so everything has to be still,
and when she has finished singing
her song goes up off the earth,
higher and higher...
till it is only as big as a tiny silver bird
with nothing but moonlight around it.

from IV
BETTY

You can see the sandhills from our new room.
Butterflies
live in the sandhills
and lizards
and centipedes.
If you keep very still
lizards will think you a stone
and run over your lap.
Butterflies' liveries
are scarlet and black.
They drive chariots in air.
People in the chariots
are pale as dew—
you can see right through them—
but the chariots
are made of gold of the sun.
They go up to heaven
and never catch fire.
There are green centipedes
and brown centipedes
and black centipedes,
because green and brown and black
are the colors in hell's flag.
Centipedes
have hundreds of feet
because it is so far from hell
to come up for air.
Centipedes
do not hurry.

They are waiting for the last day
when they will creep over the false prophets
who will have their hands tied.

: :

Night calls to the sandhills
and gathers them under her.
She pushes away cities
because their sharp lights
hurt her soft breast.
Even candles make a sore place
when they stick in the night.

There are things in the sandhills
that no one knows about...
they come out at dark when the young snakes play
and tell each other secrets
in the deaf logs.

Sometimes... before rain...
when the stars have gone inside...
the night comes close to your window
and sniffs at the light...
But you must not run away—
you must keep your face to the night
and walk backward.

: :

There are different kinds of shadows.
The blind ones
are the shadows of things.
These are the tame shadows—
they love to play on the wall with you

and follow you about like cats and dogs.
Sometimes
they hiss at you softly
like snakes that do not bite,
or swish like women's dresses,
but if you poke a candle at them
they pull in their heads and disappear.

But there is a shadow
that is not the shadow of a thing...
it is a thing itself.
When you meet this shadow
you must not look at it too long...
it grows with your looking at it...
till you are all alone
with nothing around you...
nothing... nothing... nothing...
but a shadow
with its eyes full of black light.

: :

There's a shadow in the corner of the shed,
crouching, lying in wait...
a black coiled shadow,
watching... ready to strike...
but I mustn't be afraid of it—
I mustn't be afraid of anything.
Poor evil shadow,
the candle would chase it away
only she can't get at it.

Do you think that every one hates you,
shadow with your back to the wall,

afraid to lie down and sleep?
But I don't hate you.
Even the moon means to be kind.
She just treads on you
as I'd tread on a worm that I didn't see.
Don't be afraid of me, shadow.
See—I've no light in my hand—
nothing to save myself with—
yet I walk right up to you—
if you'll let me
I'll put my arms around you
and stroke you softly.
Are you surprised I'd put my arms around you?
Is it your black black sorrow
that nobody loves you?

Jaguar

Nasal intonations of light
and clicking tongues...
publicity of windows
stoning me with pent-up cries...
smells of abattoirs...
smells of long-dead meat.

Some day-end—
while the sand is yet cozy as a blanket
off the warm body of a squaw,
and the jaguars are out to kill...
with a blue-black night coming on
and a painted cloud
stalking the first star—
I shall go alone into the Silence...
the coiled Silence...
where a cry can run only a little way
and waver and dwindle
and be lost.

And there...
where tiny antlers clinch and strain
as life grapples in a million avid points,
and threshing things
strike and die,
letting their hate live on
in the spreading purple of a wound...
I too
will make covert of a crevice in the night,
and turn and watch...
nose at the cleft's edge.

Altitude

I wonder
how it would be here with you,
where the wind
that has shaken off its dust in low valleys
touches one cleanly,
as with a new-washed hand,
and pain
is as the remote hunger of droning things,
and anger
but a little silence
sinking into the great silence.

Nocturne

Indigo bulb of darkness
Punctured by needle lights
Through a fissure of brick canyon
    shutting out stars,
And a sliver of moon
Spigoting two high windows
    over the West river...

Boy, I met to-night,
Your eyes are two red-glowing arcs
    shifting with my vision...
They reflect as in a fading proof
The deadened eyes of a woman,
And your shed virginity,
Light as the withered pod of a sweet pea,
Moist and fragrant
Blows against my soul.
What are you to me, boy,
That I, who have passed so many lights,
Should carry your eyes
Like swinging lanterns?

Time-Stone

Hallo, Metropolitan—
Ubiquitous windows staring all ways,
Red eye notching the darkness.
No use to ogle that slip of a moon.
This midnight the moon,
Playing virgin after all her encounters,
Will break another date with you.
You fuss an awful lot,
You flight of ledger books,
Overrun with multiple ant-black figures
Dancing on spindle legs
An interminable can-can.
But I'd rather... like the cats in the alley... count time
By the silver whistle of a moonbeam
Falling between my stoop-shouldered walls,
Than all your tally of the sunsets,
Metropolitan, ticking among stars.

Wall Street at Night

Long vast shapes... cooled and flushed through with
darkness...
Lidless windows
Glazed with a flashy luster
From some little pert café chirping up like a sparrow.
And down among iron guts
Piled silver
Throwing gray spatter of light... pale without heat...
Like the pallor of dead bodies.

East River

Dour river
Jaded with monotony of lights
Diving off mast heads...
Lights mad with creating in a river... turning its sullen
    back...
Heave up, river...
Vomit back into the darkness your spawn of light...
The night will gut what you give her.

Sons of Belial

I

We are old,
Old as song.
Before Rome was
Or Cyrene.
Mad nights knew us
And old men's wives.
We knew who spilled the sacred oil
For young-gold harlots of the town....
We knew where the peacocks went
And the white doe for sacrifice.

II

We were the sons of Belial.
One black night
Centuries ago
We beat at a door
In Gilead....
We took the Levite's concubine
We plucked her hands from off the door....
We choked the cry into her throat
And stuck the stars among her hair....
We glimpsed the madly swaying stars
Between the rhythms of her hair...
And all our mute and separate strings
Swelled in a raging symphony....

Our blood sang pæans
All that night
Till dawn fell like a wounded swan
Upon the fields of Gilead.

III

We are old....
Old as song....
We are dumb song.
(Epics tingled
In our blood
When we haled Hypatia
Over the stones
In Alexandria.)

Could we loose
The wild rhythms clinched in us....
March in bands of troubadours....
We would be of gentle mood.
When Christ healed us
Who were dumb—
When he freed our shut-in song—
We strewed green palms
At his pale feet...
We sang hosannas
In Jerusalem.
And all our fumbling voices blent
In a brief white harmony.
(But a mightier song
Was in us pent

When we nailed Christ
To a four-armed tree.)

IV

We are young.
When we rise up with singing roots,
(Warm rains washing
Gutters of Berlin
Where we stamped Rosa... Luxemburg
On a night in spring.)
Rhythms skurry in our blood.
Little nimble rats of song
In our feet run crazily
And all is dust... we trample... on.

Mad nights when we make ritual
(Feet running before the sleuth-light...
And the smell of burnt flesh
By a flame-ringed hut
In Missouri,
Sweet as on Rome's pyre....)
We make ropes do rigadoons
With copper feet that jig on air....

We are the Mob....
Old as song,
Tyre knew us
And Israel.

In Harness

I

The foreman's head
slowly circling...
White rims
under yellow disks of eyes...
Gold hairs
starting out of a blond scowl...
Hovering... disappearing... recurring...
the foreman's head.

Droning of power-machines...
droning of girl with adenoids...
Arms flapping with a fin-like motion
under sun burning down through a sky-light like a glass lid.
Light skating on the rims of wheels...
boring in gimlet points.
Needles flickering
fierce white threads of light
fine as a wasp's sting.
Light in sweat-drops brighter than eyes
and calico-pallid faces
and bodies throwing off smells—
and the air a bloated presence
    pressing on the walls
and the silence a compressed scream.

Allons enfants de la patrie—
Electric... piercing... shrill as a fife
the voice of a little Russian

breaks out of the shivered circle.
Another voice rises... another and another
leaps like flame to flame.
And life—surging, clamorous, swarming like a rabble
    crazily fluttering ragged petticoats—
comes rushing back into torpid eyes
like suddenly yielded gates.

The girl with adenoids
rocks on her hams.
A torrent of song
strains at her throat,
gurgles, rushes, gouges her blocked pipes.
Her feet beat a wild tattoo—
head flung back and pelvis lifting
to the white body of the sun.
Mates now, these two—
goddess and god...
Marchons!

Only the power machines drone
with metallic docility
under the flaxen head of the foreman
poised like an amazed gull.

II

To-day
little French merchant men
with pointed beards
and fat American merchant men
without any beards

drive to a feast of buttered squabs.
The band... accoutered and neatly caparisoned... plays the
    Marseillaise...
And I think of a wild stallion... newly caught...
flanks yet taut and nostrils spread
to the smell of a racing mare,
hitched to a grocer's cart.

To Alexander Berkman

Can you see me, Sasha?
I can see you...
A tentacle of the vast dawn is resting on your face
that floats as though detached
in a sultry and greenish vapor.
I cannot reach my hands to you...
would not if I could,
though I know how warmly yours would close about them.
Why?
I do not know...
I have a sense of shame.
Your eyes hurt me... mysterious openings in the gray
  stone of your face
through which your spirit streams out taut as a flag
bearing strange symbols to the new dawn.

If I stay... projected, trembling against these bars filtering
  emaciated light...
will your eyes... that bore their lonely way through mine...
stop as at a friendly gate...
grow warm... and luminous?
... but I cannot stay... for the smell...
I know... how the days pass...
The prison squats
with granite haunches
on the young spring,
battened under with its twisting green...

and you... socket for every bolt
piercing like a driven nail.
Eyes stare you through the bars...
eyes blank as a graveled yard...
and the silence shuffles heavy dice of feet in iron corridors...
until the day... that has soiled herself in this black hole
to caress the pale mask of your face...
withdraws the last wizened ray
to wash in the infinite
her discolored hands.
Can you hear me, Sasha,
in your surrounded darkness?

Emma Goldman

How should they appraise you,
who walk up close to you
as to a mountain,
each proclaiming his own eyeful
against the other's eyeful.

Only time
standing well off
shall measure your circumference
        and height.

To Larkin

Is it you I see go by the window, Jim Larkin—you not
 looking at me nor any one,
And your shadow swaying from East to West?
Strange that you should be walking free—you shut down
 without light,
And your legs tied up with a knot of iron.

One hundred million men and women go inevitably about
 their affairs,
In the somnolent way
Of men before a great drunkenness…
They do not see you go by their windows, Jim Larkin,
With your eyes bloody as the sunset
And your shadow gaunt upon the sky…
You, and the like of you, that life
Is crushing for their frantic wines.

Wind Rising in the Alleys

Wind rising in the alleys
My spirit lifts in you like a banner
  streaming free of hot walls.
You are full of unspent dreams...
You are laden with beginnings...
There is hope in you... not sweet...
  acrid as blood in the mouth.
Come into my tossing dust
Scattering the peace of old deaths,
Wind rising in the alleys,
Carrying stuff of flame.

RED FLAG

(1927)

Mo-ti

You talked in mellow day-ends
as the rallying sun
spread quivering spokes of gold
like an iridescent fan behind the pagodas,
and smells of bamboo shoots cooked in spices
drifted out of the blown fires.

You pitted your words against the words of princes,
but softly, in even tones, and few listened...
so that you were not nailed on four boards
nor smeared with honey and left naked
where sands crawl living under the sun.

Perhaps only a few boys listened
while the rice was cooling in the bowls
and auburn sunsets
changing into lavender and jade
shuffled into the lilac dusks.
A few boys listen always when one gives out of his silence.

I do not think there were girls who listened...
girls... whose lustrous pale skins
threw back in dusky echoes
the faint gold light of evening
that loitered with silken slippers upon the pinnacles.

Not so could you have touched their deep quietness,
incomprehensible, moving darkly
under the froth of little words
and the soft purling of their blood

that perhaps sang to meet your blood...
you passed them all unknowing
while the light on the horizon was like a topaz wine.

Did women—scattering dry words
as trees dead leaves,
that are no more communicants of the green sap—
women with shining secrets in their eyes...
alertly curious eyes
not baffled because not wondering...
catch a garbled word or so
and mutely
quiver along the margins of their silences?

Not again, Mo-ti,
when heated days turn yellow at the edges,
and the sun comes down like a peacock to drink out of the
 rivers,
will lemon-pale boys,
pressed against the narrow darkness of their eyes
bring to you their spindling hungers...
(what becomes of all the boys who have touched silence for a
 white shaken moment...
does the shy wild light that comes into their eyes
there beat itself out like a too long shut-in thing?)
I do not know if they talked with you in those gone saffron
 twilights.
Only your
words have floated out of the night,
 enfolding them and you in its seamless shadow...
words still seeking in vain noise
for some green hush to rest upon...
words carrying light like sunsets upon wings.

Death Ray

I

There is that in the air, an imminence
Of things that hold the breath still and heart pale;
Nought that the mind affirms, but a fey sense
Illumines, and goes dark. Can it avail
For men to follow what but dreams have had
In high and secret places—the dim torch
That Zarathustra blew on and went mad.

Was this the gleam that Jesus sought by night,
When he walked, veiled... in glamorous dim light
Washed, as a white goat before the slaughter...
And heard no sound save the soft rhythmic beat
Upon the silken silence of his feet
Beautiful as gulls upon the water.

II

A joy is in the morning, veiled…
a light within a light…
now on the brick wall that burns to rose
and all but pulsates, now a gleam
as of a white soaring bird
that eyes strain for and lose sight…
now in a nimbus as of steam,
surrounding a clear flame,
invisible.

A joy floats in the morning, veiled…
a light within a light
that draws the trembling spirit like a seed…
a splendour in the morning, imminent,
a stirring at the quick
of some white palpitating core
of such intensity as might
burn up Manhattan like a reed.

III

Dawn is like a broken honeycomb
spilling over the waxen edges of the clouds
  that drip with light...
spires, swarming up the mauve mist,
reach their rosy tips
like little pointed tongues
first about a shining platter,
and every window is a brazier
that cups the living gold.

Even the squat chimneys,
rooting heaven,
catch the sun upon their snouts
  and keep it balancing.

Only my heart
like a splintered vase
is envious of the light
it cannot hold.

IV

Balance a sunbeam as you would a jar
Filled with clear water where no waters are...
Let not slip silently back in the sun,
There to be as in a field no more than one
of many dandelions... this nuclear
Period set against the rushing hour
That holds there, motionless, the leaning sheer
Stalk of its unfathomable flower.

Let pass into the night its shining band,
So that they leave the covenant in your hand
Of lighted water, and the prideful calm
Of hilltops in most high untaken air:
Yet know that there shall cleave forever there
A golden nailhead, burning in your palm.

The Fifth-Floor Window

Walls... iridescent with eyes
that stare into the courtyard
at the still thing lying
in the turned-back snow...
stark precipice of walls
with a foam of white faces
lathering their stone lips...
faces of the shawled women
the walls pour forth without aim
under the vast pallor of the sky.

They point at the fifth-floor window
and whisper one to the other:
"It's hard on a man out of work
an' the mother gone out of his door
with a younger lover..."

The blanched morning stares
in like a face flattened against the pane
where the little girl used to cry all day
with a feeble and goading cry.
Her father, with his eyes at bay
before the vague question of the light,
says that she fell...
Between his twitching lips
a stump of cigarette
smoulders, like a burning root.

Only the wind was abroad
in high cold hours
of the icy and sightless night
with back to the stars—
night growing white and still as a pillar of salt
and the snow mushing without sound—
when something hurtled through the night
and drifted like a larger snow-flake
in the trek of the blind snow
that stumbled over it in heaps—
only white-furred wind
pawed at the fifth-floor window
and nosed cigarette-butts on the sill...
till the window closed down softly
on the silvery fleece of wind
that tore and left behind its flying fringes.

Now the wind
down the valley of the tenements
sweeps in weakened rushes
and meddles with the clothes-lines
where little white pinafores sway stiffly
like dead geese.
Over the back-yards
that are laid out smooth and handsome as a corpse
under the seamless snow,
the sky is a vast ash-pit
where the buried sun
rankles in a livid spot.

Red Flag

Red flag waving over Spartacus,
Red cloth stripped from a gladiator's loins
To flutter in the milk-warm wind along the roads of Capua,
Red flag shaken like a bloody hand in the face of kings...
Red clout stuck on a spike—
There flaunting gay as a red rose pinned
On a beggar's cap in London Town—
Or clenched in a maimed hand...
A red and a white rose smashed together...
Red shoots mauled and trodden yet ever sprouting anew
Till the lopped staff blooms again...
Red flower of the barricades—
First over the scarp and last left lying
  like spat-up blood upon the snow,
When ice-fangs bristle in the cooled-off guns
And dawn creeps in between the forepaws of the silence
  that crouches above the dead...

Red light burning down the centuries...
Red fire dwindling to a spark but never out...
Gleaming a moment on Bunker Hill... sinking,
  a blown-out flame,
  leaving a deeper greyness...
Red Flag over the domes of Moscow...
There gleaming like a youth's shed blood on gold
Red flag kerchief of the sun—
Over devastation I salute you.

Libation

The soldiers lie upon the snow
that no longer gyrates under the spinning lights,
night juggles in her fat black hands.
They will not babble any more secrets to loose-mouthed nights,
   expanding in golden auras,
while sleigh-bells jingle like new coins, the darkness shuffles...
They will not drink any more wine—
wine of the Romanoffs',
jewelled wine,
the secret years worked slowly at
till it was wrought to fire,
as stones are faceted
until they give out light.
The soldiers lie very still.
Their shadows have shrunk up close
as toads shrink under a stone,
and night and silence...
the ancient cronies...
foregather about them.

But still over the snow that is white as a ram's fleece
arms swing like scythes...
and shadows in austere lines
sway in a monstrous and mysterious ritual—
shadows of the Kronstad sailors
pouring blood and wine...
   wine
spurting out of flagons in a spray of amethyst
   and gold

creeping in purple sluices,
   wine
and blood in thin bright streams
besprinkling the immaculate snow,
   blood
high-powered with heat of old vineyards
boring... into the cool snow...
blood and wine
mingling in bright pools
that suck at the lights of Petrograd
as dying eyes
suck in their last sunset.

The night has a rare savour,
out of the snow piles... altar-high
and coloured as by a rosy sacrifice...
scented vapour
ascends in a pale incense...
faint astringent perfume
of blood and wine.

Easter Morning

They bring—while fields are chiming with soft notes
Of the arisen lilies—from white pods
Smell-less offerings to anæmic gods;
As earth, resurgent, trumpets at their throats
To hail her gods of the first dark surmise—
Who parted waters with a glistening tusk
And came out with the privy stars at dusk
To trouble rivers with their small fierce eyes.

They gather at the cross, whose haggard sign
Impends in the moon-ushered dawn that leans—
In rose and ivory on tender greens
Of new corn covering an old design—
To light the brown rapt faces who kept tryst
With all the dark bright gods that they name Christ.

South-East Wind

There is remembered terror in your touch
Of spruce and palm and cedar—the wild trees
That strain against the dawns. Drained life of these
You carry, that have tamed a million such—
You that have outlived ruth and known the wills
Of seas on islands, too alone with them,
And heard men cry out on their gods to stem
Earth, unanimous, rising from the hills...
And clawed moon-harried tides throughout the wide
Low-swinging night... breaking the long stride
Of stars. You know of old harsh remedies,
Wind... cleansed of salt, with delicate cool tips
Light as a blind girl's fingers on the lips...
And bitter healing at the roots of seas.

Electrocution

He shudders... feeling on the shaven spot
The probing wind, that stabs him to a thought
Of storm-drenched fields in a white foam of light,
And roads of his hill-town that leap to sight
Like threads of tortured silver... while the guards—
Monstrous deft dolls that move as on a string,
In wonted haste to finish with this thing,
Turn faces blanker than asphalted yards.

They heard the shriek that tore out of its sheath
But as a feeble moan... yet dared not breathe,
Who stared there at him, arching—like a tree
When the winds wrench it and the earth holds tight—
Whose soul, expanding in white agony,
Had fused in flaming circuit with the night.

Morning Ride

Headlines chanting—
  youth
  lynched ten years ago
                        cleared—
  Skyscrapers
  seeming still
  whirling on their concrete
  bases,
  windows
  fanged—
  leo frank
  lynched ten
      say it with flowers
  wrigley's spearmint gum
      carter's little liver—
  lean
  to the soft blarney of the wind
  fooling with your hair,
  look
  milk-clouds oozing over the blue
      Step Lively Please
      Let 'Em Out First Let 'Em Out
  did he too feel it on his forehead,
  the gentle raillery of the wind,
  as the rope pulled taut over the tree
  in the cool dawn?

Kelvin Barry

You that walked with your head held high,
Shining and tall and straight, in the trampled morning,
Did your red young mouth
Suck in the wind as a lover sucks in a kiss that is one of the last,
As you walked with the pride in your heart
And your bare throat warm to the wishful rope
(Tighter than arm of woman was the hairy kiss of the rope),
And your face held still and high
Like a flaming lily of Saint Joseph
In the cool blue of the morning.

ANNUNIATION

But for the violets...
and earth a gigantic bulb battened down with stone...
violets
at which the wind
makes little shambling rushes,
unsteady wind,
milk-warm and dewy at the mouth,
stumbling and rising again,
smelling of the violets...
and but for the wind
scattering
such scented hearsay,
one might not veer
on this unleavened stone
to the sharp pull of earth
at tension with the violets—
one might hurry on unknowing over the cancelled spring,
spring... horned green
and curly as a ram's head...
desperately butting against the concrete.

Obliteration

The sea is a wrinkled silence
Moving darkly
Under the audacious lustre of the air…
The emptily effacing air,
That has closed upon so many cries…
Yet holds in its blue vacuum
No bleached white evidence.

Timeline

1873 Lola Ridge is born in Dublin, Ireland, as Rose Emily Ridge on December 12. Ridge and her mother move to New Zealand after Ridge's father dies.

1880 Ridge's mother remarries a Scottish miner, a passionate man who quoted Shakespeare and who was violent when drunk.

1895 Ridge marries Peter Webster, the manager of a gold mine. Her first son is born the following year and lives less than two weeks.

1900 Her second son, Keith, is born.

1903–1907 Ridge's marriage to Webster falls apart and she, her son, and her mother move to Australia, where Ridge studies painting at the Academie Julienne and at Trinity College in Sydney, New South Wales. She writes her first book, *Verses*, which remains unpublished.

1907–1918 Ridge's mother dies and Ridge immigrates to the United States, landing in San Francisco, where she stays for a short time, then moves on to New York. The first few years after Ridge came to the States, she supports herself by working as an illustrator, factory worker, poet, and model. She starts attending meetings of the Ferrer Association, an utopian anarchist organization, and gets involved in labor activism.

1918 B. W. Huebsch publishes Ridge's book, *The Ghetto and Other Poems*.

1919 Ridge marries a second time, to David Lawson. She gives her lecture, "Woman and the Creative Will," arguing against biological destiny. She serves as associate editor of the literary magazine *Others*.

1920 B. W. Huebsch publishes Ridge's second book, *Sun-Up and Other Poems*.

1922–3 She serves as American editor for the literary magazine *Broom*.

1927 Viking publishes *Red Flag*. Ridge is arrested in Boston for protesting the executions of the anarchists Sacco and Vanzetti.

1929 Payson & Clarke publishes *Firehead*.

1935 Ridge wins the Shelley Memorial Award for poetry and a Guggenheim Poetry Fellowship. Harrison Smith and Robert Haas, Publishers, issues *Dance of Fire*, Ridge's last book.

1936 Ridge again wins the Shelley Memorial Award for poetry.

1941 Ridge dies on May 19 in Brooklyn, New York, from acute pulmonary tuberculosis.

Notes on the Poems

The Ghetto
Johann Caspar Schmidt was a nineteenth-century German philosopher who wrote under the name of Max Stirner. His most famous book, *The Ego and Its Own,* had a profound effect on Karl Marx's thinking.

Frank Little on Calvary
In 1917, Frank Little was leading miners in Butte, Montana, in a strike against the Anaconda Company. On August 1, some men broke into his hotel room as he slept, beat him up, tied him to a car and dragged him out of town. His body was found in the morning hanging from a railroad trestle with a note threatening other strike organizers.

Sons of Belial
Rosa Luxemburg was a Polish Jew who was an active Marxist theorist and revolutionary in Germany. She was imprisoned for her activities a number of times. She took part in the German uprisings against the First World War and was killed by members of the Freikorps, a German paramilitary organization, on January 15, 1919.

To Alexander Berkman
Alexander Berkman was the son of a wealthy Jewish businessman. In 1887, he emigrated from Russia to the United States where he became an active anarchist. In 1922, he attempted to assassinate Henry Clay Frick, a wealthy industrialist, and for which he was imprisoned. He wrote a number of books on politics and anarchism and worked on Emma Goldman's (with whom he was romantically involved) newspaper, *Mother Earth.* He founded the Ferrer Center, an anarchist society. In terrible pain from a chronic illness, he shot and killed himself on June 28, 1936.

Emma Goldman
Emma Goldman was born to a Jewish family in Lithuania in 1869. She emigrated to the United States when she was 17. Noting the conditions of workers, she quickly became an anarchist and revolutionary. She became romatically involved with Alexander Berkman and plotted, with him, to assassinate Henry Clay Frick. When the assassination attempt did not succeed, Berkman refused to implicate Goldman.

Jailed for her activities a number of times, she was deported to Russia in 1919. She spent time in Russia, England, and France. She went to Spain and supported the Republic during the Spanish Civil War.

To Larkin

James Larkin was an Irish labor organizer and socialist activist. Known as "Big Jim," he played a key role in the Dublin Lockout in 1913 and his activities were instrumental in the formation of the new Irish Free State. In 1914, he left Ireland for the United States, where he continued his socialist activism. His "criminal anarchy" got him imprisoned in 1920 and ultimately deported back to Ireland in 1923. He continued his labor and socialist activism in Ireland and won election several times to the Dáil (Irish Parliament).

Libation

In March 1921, Russian sailors at the Kronstad (more commonly spelled Kronstadt) naval base in the Gulf of Finland rebelled against Bolshevik rule, specifically against Soviet economic policy. The uprising was bloodily put down by the Red Army.

Kelvin Barry

In *Red Flag*, Lola Ridge inserted the following note on this poem: "Kelvin Barry was an Irish boy of eighteen, who, some time after the Easter Rebellion, took part in a demonstration in which one or two of the Army of Occupation were shot. The British were so impressed with his youth and the courage of his bearing that they offered him his life and liberty if he would reveal the identity of his comrades. He proudly refused and was hanged. The priest who witnessed the hanging said he had never seen a man die more bravely." His name is more commonly spelled as Kevin Barry.

quale [kwa-lay]: *Eng. n* 1. A property (such as hardness) considered apart from things that have that property. 2. A property that is experienced as distinct from any source it may have in a physical object. *Ital. pron.a.* 1. Which, what. 2. Who. 3. Some. 4. As, just as.

Made in the USA